AFRICAN WRITERS SERIES
Editorial Adviser · Chinua Achebe

42

# MESSAGES

*Poems from Ghana*

# AFRICAN WRITERS SERIES

# MESSAGES
## Poems from Ghana

Edited by
Kofi Awoonor
& G. Adali-Mortty

HEINEMANN
LONDON · IBADAN · NAIROBI

Heinemann Educational Books
48 Charles Street London WIX8AH
PMB 5205 Ibadan · POB 25080 Nairobi
EDINBURGH MELBOURNE TORONTO
AUCKLAND HONG KONG SINGAPORE

ISBN 0 435 90042 0

Set in Monotype Baskerville and
Printed in Great Britain by
Cox & Wyman Ltd, London, Fakenham and Reading

# CONTENTS

# CONTENTS

# CONTENTS

# CONTENTS

## CONTENTS

JOE DE GRAFT *The Gene*


Time went to dine with Science
And rose reeling from draughts of human blood,
A crimson ulcer flaming on his chromosome.

This is the hush hour before the holocaust:
You
And me
And you –
Victims patiently waiting
To be slaughtered upon decadent altars
For worlds already septic in the womb.

Who will redeem the future?
Time is a hermaphrodite,
And the ulcer burns crimson on her chromosome.

At the end of this slip-way,
Beyond the foaming breakers,
The old sailing ships used to rest
Preening their white wings in the breeze
As they waited for their cargo.

Look now, how the green sea-weed
Covers all the slip-way!

Now feel,
Feel with the sole of your infant feet
The fierce dragon rock beneath the silken weed,
Teeth-of-dragon rock stained red-brown
As with ancient blood –
Blood not all the waters of the sea can wash away.

Then look across the ocean;
Look beyond the breakers,
Far out beyond the curve
Of meeting sky and ocean,
And tell me what you see.

Nothing?

Yet in those ancestral days
There was a chain –
A chain of flesh and iron wrought;
And it held beyond this slip-way,
Reaching out to sea
Far, far beyond the curve
Of meeting sky and ocean,
On to the other side of the Atlantic.

[2]

They say the guinea-fowl lays her treasure
Where only she can find it.
Akosua 'Nowa is a guinea-fowl:
Go tell her, red ant upon the tree.

I met Akosua 'Nowa this morning;
I greeted:
   Akosua, how is your treasure?
She looked me slowly up and down,
She sneered:
   The man is not yet here who'll find it!

Akosua 'Nowa has touched my manhood;
Tell her, red ant upon the tree:
If she passes this way I am gone,
I am gone to load my gun.

No matter how hidden deep her treasure,
By my father's coffin I swear
I'll shoot my way to it this day;
Son of the hunter king
   There is liquid fire in my gun!

I am looking through the window
    At the soldiers marching past.
They are singing, lustily,
    About a man with a penis like a cannon
    And a woman who . . .
But no matter; the songs may be obscene
But everybody is happy, today being anniversary,
And that's all that matters, come to think of it.

The side-walks are jammed.
The people are cheering the soldiers,
Women spreading their cloth on the tarmac
    For the heroes to march on;
And the men too –
    Even those who cursed bitterly that day
    Because their picnic had been so abruptly stopped –
They are all cheering wildly.
This is the anniversary of the revolution.

A-a-ah! Here comes the commander,
    Riding on his jeep.
He is waving to us
He is waving to everybody,
And they are wild, really wild – cheering!
    You can hear them, can't you?
What a wonderful day!
And what a fine man the commander!
He is a fine man,
    Honest, brave and modest;
Long live the commander!
He's cut just right for the presidency,
    Don't you think?

[4]

JOE DE GRAFT

Yes, we'll make him president,
Long live the commander!

All this was only a year ago.
The columns of marching soldiers
    The cheering crowds
        The banners and bunting . . .
You wouldn't believe it, only a year ago.
But what a year!
    Because during this year we –
    Well, to cut a long story short,
    We went civilian.

And today is anniversary day again
And I am looking through the window.
    No soldiers march along the streets
    No obscene songs
        About a man with a member like . . .
But no matter;
Let us rejoice, everybody who can,
For that's all that matters, come to think of it.

The crowds are out again.
Thousands of men on the side-walks,
And the office windows jammed to the top-most floors –
    White-shirted office clerks cheering!
And the women in the streets
    As usual,
    This time demanding redress,
    Proscription of all who took part in
        The exercise that turned into the operation
        That put a stop to the picnic!

[5]

Fat-bottomed women, over-dressed and be-powdered,
  Screaming termagants.
I assure you,
  Whoever writes the future history of this land
  will deserve a lynching if he underestimates the
  contribution of our women to the development of
  political consciousness and the establishment
  of the State!

To tell the truth
There has been another revolution, man,
And this is a demonstration
  Of the masses,
  Seething mile upon mile of them.
Look now who comes riding on a jeep, waving to us -
  Not old Moke?!
I tell you, man,
  The old gang's all here!
    'Forward ever backward never'
    'Beep-beep-beep, wɔbɛkɔ assembly'
    'There is victory for us'
    'Down with the opposition' . . .
And the people are wild, really wild –
Cheering and cheering from the windows;
What a wonderful day!
What a really wonderful day!

As for the commander –
Well, to cut a long story short,
  We went civilian!
  And friends still in touch with him say he is
  Convalescing from the shock.

[6]

As everybody knows,
 He lost the election to **Kwame** *in absentia!*

And now the people want their old messiah back.

In parliament tonight they are debating a new bill
 introduced by one of our veteran politicians,
 a man they locked up the day the picnic was
 interrupted.
  (Apart from the big part he had played helping
  to build up the old party on foundations of
  unquestionable infallibility, and his contribu-
  tion to the formulation and operation of the
  Detention Act, he had at one time been master
  of the revels, which meant power to sink
  millions of our money into champagne and caviar
  and things of that sort. He also had been found
  by a Commission of Enquiry to be heavily
  involved in . . . But why should I bother good
  citizens with facts everybody knows?)
 It is an interesting bill, to say the least.
 Tonight is the final reading,
 And by all accounts it is going to go through
 Without opposition.
 . . . Abolition of all political elections . . .
  Substitution of the Central Committee for the
   Cabinet . . .
  Presidential prerogatives in all matters judicial . . .
  Infallibility of the party . . .
  Life tenure of the presidency . . .
  Etc., etc., etc.
The new deal is in,

[7]

And we are back where we were interrupted –
In the middle of the picnic.

This is a big demonstration, man,
And the cheering is deafening!
I see some chiefs over there, on the side-walk;
The crowd is giving them a tough time,
Pressing them into a corner, pressing;
And they look bewildered;
   But that's nothing new: Chiefs?
   They have been bewildered these fifty years and more
   Except, of course,
   Where they've seen a clear advantage to themselves,
   Then they've acted with decision
   As in this revolution.
   These bewildered chiefs are the few without guts;
   All the others defected long ago
   To the side of the majority in parliament:
   That's where the cedis are!

I do not see any civil servants in the crush.
Poor devils,
   *Their* picnic is over, as they very well know,
   And they are *back* at the wheel,
   Obediently and faithfully steering the old ship
     To perdition!

As to the intellectuals –
Well, again the same old story:
   The smart lawyers among them
     Quickly diagnosed the new developments,

[8]

And are calmly piling it up in the banks
While the going is good,
In the name of the Law and the Constitution;
A few of the university ones
  Got themselves professorships abroad
  For their learned analyses
  Of the many things that went wrong;
Some, like the chiefs,
  Threw in their lot with the new majority
    in parliament,
  And are earning quite decent salaries
  And a growing reputation
  As oracles of the new deal;
Others, the largest percentage naturally,
  No less milky in the liver
  Than any nine hundred and ninety-nine
  Out of a thousand men,
  Are quietly towing the line
    For dear academic comfort
    And a well-earned superannuation;
Of those remaining,
  Some are gone stark mad,
  While the final few, though sane,
  Admit that they are impotent;
  Which, in a situation like the present,
    Would be natural
  Even if they carried cannon between their legs!

So here I am this morning
Early in the kitchen.

The aroma of fresh coffee on the boil,
   Nose-filling aroma of good fresh coffee
     on the boil;
  And this kitchen is good to be in
  And good to hear the browning water
     babble-bubbling inside the glass-trap
     head of the percolator;
And the good wife still asleep in her vono bed
Dreaming good dreams, I hope,
Of me!

All night the tummy hasn't been well,
   Running like it wanted nothing more
     to do with me for eating what I
     do not know –
  All night a running tummy;
  Till at last out of weariness
  I drop into oblivion between 4 and 5
  Quite unknowing –
    Deep oblivion
    Sweet as feathers . . .

Then crash out of nowhere
The white day comes bursting in
  Through frosted louvres . . .

And it's good to be alive!

Good indeed to be alive,
   So thank we god
   For everything,
      And the myriad sparrows
      Chirruping in the fresh morning sun outside
      While the percolator bubbles.

And here a loaf of bread
And there a jar of marmalade
And sugar for the dreaming wife
And milk just turned out of its blue tin
   now rolling
      on its back
   like a cat,
And there the frying-pan on the gas cooker
   And two eggs spluttering away –
   Yolk of golden egg with garnishing of
      onion and new-cut pepper green and
      winking red,
And a little salt
   A little salt . . .

Oh damn!
A hot speck of spitting oil near got me
In the eye.

Yes reader
What d'you say?

Oh, mustn't I?
  Mustn't drink good coffee in the
    morning,
  Mustn't eat good bread and marmalade
    for breakfast,
  Mustn't fry eggs over a gas cooker
    While my good wife
    Still lies dreaming,
And mustn't read books, I suppose,
Nor write poetry,
  Because –
What d'you say?
  Because
  Not African!

But listen
The radio in my sitting-room
(I should have told you of the radio):
Listen –
  Drum sounds on *15 megacycles*
  Signalling the new day in Africa,
  Pop sounds
  Calling the waking continent
  To the Breakfast Show,
  Many-tongued voices
Daring all men everywhere
    To breathe in the dawn-fresh winds
    Blowing across a changing world.

And the warrior chieftains pass on
And the beaded maidens dance away

[12]

And we sit by the running waters
  And sigh for an innocence that is gone.

But here –
  The eggs are done;

And still it's good to be alive!

And though I cannot whistle out loud
I know there is joy
  Bubbling like coffee inside me,
Sweet aromatic joy
  Of being alive,
  So thank we god
    For everything
    And the myriad sparrows
    Chirruping in the fresh morning sun outside
    While the percolator babbles,
And I feel coming alive within me
The first movement of an un-African poem.

Do not tell me, friend,
How much your feet itch
To take the footpath
Out of this forest clearing
   Where nothing stirs
   But the leaves protesting
     against the world-ranging wind's
     constant teasing;
   And the weaver birds returning
     for a while to breed in the
     sunset branches
     And off again to-morrow's season;
   And the streaked barn-mouse content to live
     its tremulous days among the husks
     of last year's harvest;
Do not tell me, friend.


Looking into your eyes
I can tell –
   Your yearning for the world beyond,
   Your brave dreams
   Of towns and cities awaiting conquest, yielding
     Their wealth of work
     And exotic women's love
     And acclaim for wondrous deeds
     Never before done by man.
Looking into your eyes
I know.


But I know too, that once
One young like you

[14]

Dreamed like you
And yearned:


The footpath opened out into the road,
The road into the towns,
And thence –
   The wide sea's trackless way,
   The expanding universe above sun-bleached clouds –
To fabulous cities founded on gold.


In the forest clearing
   The weaver birds knew his presence:
   Their querulous cries would stop
   And then begin again
      In salutation
      Of another nature's creature.
   The leaves smelt fresh above him
   And oozed sweet sap beneath his tread;
   And when night came
      The earth breathed upon his rest,
      The stars drew near.


Now –
A ceaseless roar of machines,
   Metal gods
   That acknowledged not his presence
   But demanded endless service;
And disembodied voices flying on the air
   Whirled round and round his ears –
   Incessant din of rumours and alarms;

He sought consolation
   In the arms of one he met
   On his wanderings.
Engulfed within her soft embrace
   He dreamt
   He had found the stillness
      Of the forest clearing he knew;
But the eyes that had beckoned him with their calm
   Suddenly stared back flat and scared:
      In their pupils he glimpsed a horror spreading,
   And all around him –
      Throngs of rest-forsaken humanity.

His feet grew wings;
But perched atop the tallest edifice of all
At last his heart misgave him:
   Though high above the world
      No nearer was he to the stars;
   Miles below him
      Life roared on
      And still there was great stir;
      And men,
      Grown smaller now than mice,
      Raced round, about their narrow business
         Among the debris
         Of a synthetic
         Unsympathetic world.

Silver dewdrops sparkling in the dawn:
Budding dimples smiling in thesunrise

    Tell me, good mother, tell me
    Who shall my husband be?

        Prince shall he be and handsome,
        Feet befitting golden sandals,
        Chaplet on his brow of camel weave,
        And he shall come in the prime of noon.

Golden shadows racing in the sunset
Wispy tresses trembling in the dusk:

        Sigh not, lonely heart, sigh not
        The day will soon be gone.

    I've waited and waited and waited
    Till my eyes begin to droop;
    Now my prince comes o'er the horizon
    And at my door
        Death's decked palanquin.

JOE DE GRAFT *Japhy Ryder: Dharma Bum*
[*To Jack Kerouac*]

There go the dogs again,
I wonder what's the matter this time?

    Oh nothing, my dear;
    Only Zen Lunatic Japhy
    Passing along on human feet,
    His rucksack on his back.

Poor poor Japhy!
It's so chilly-dark outside
But warm in here and cosy too;
Shall we ask him in to view with us
And a cup of coffee maybe?

    You may if you fancy, my dear,
    Only – you don't know Japhy.
    His eyes are on the stars
    His feet on snow-bound Matterhorn
    His soul ecstatic in distant Japan
        Sipping tea with old Zen masters.
    He owns no TV nor a house,
    And the neighbourhood dogs may growl at him
        For coming by on human feet,
    But he's richer-happier far than we, my dear,
        Because
        He's set on his way to the Dharma.

JOE DE GRAFT *Footsteps*
[*To L.*]

Five o'clock,
Footsteps on the veranda –
Clear, ringing steps
Light and thrilling.

I see them: shapely little feet;
They come tap . . . tap . . . tapping
Nearer and nearer
Upon the cement floor,
Upon the threshold of my heart.

Dainty little feet
In little black suede shoes,
High heels not so high,
Erect without effort.

I feel them: steady little feet;
They come pat . . . pat . . . patting
Along the strings of my heart,
Deeper and deeper
Into my lonely life.

Little feet, I cannot stop you;
Little feet, *Akwaaba!*

You took my man away;
In the mid-bloom of my marriage morn
You took my man away.

When I came questing at your door
You had him yoked in honey toil
When I came questing at your door.

You turned your lock upon my face
And sneered he shall not come to me,
You turned your lock upon my face;

And –

He laughed I would not come again,
The love-pang twisting at my heart
He laughed I would not come again.

   I have been on a long, long journey;
   I have been among the northern hills
   Where the red god broods in his cave;
   I have been among the hills of Tongo.

Though you possess my man every hour,
His soul that I have drunk
In three draughts with white kola
Deep in the caves of Tongo –
That cannot you possess,
Not if you sprout ten thousand talons
To clutch him to your breast.

   And –

Oh he shall come to me
And I shall receive him
Not once nor seventy times,
But whenever in the hold of your grasping love-lips
The wild shudders shake him:
'Tis me shall receive his liquid ecstasies –
Me you sneered away in the morning,
Me
His woman returned from Tongo.

It's three in the middle of the night and I'm
   lying in bed reading about
   This man.
And I think to myself he must have had something –
   This man.

A VC 10 suddenly comes to life two miles away at the
   airport
   And the booming waves fill the night
   Brim over
      flooding the world
      rising to a monstrous roar
   Then recede with a drone . . .
Perhaps a direct flight to Johannesburg.

And I am alone again in a silent world
   Alone reading in a world asleep,
So innocently breathing in its sleep
   You wouldn't think
   It could be so cruel to any man –

This man who had something to say that would not
   be listened to,
   and so
*He died the day the banning order was served on him.*

I am lying in bed
Wide awake
Middle of the night
Cannot sleep.

JOE DE GRAFT

Now then, listen, *you old bastard*
    (wherever you are):
Though I've never met you beyond a few
    written scraps about you,
Nor will ever possibly come anywhere near
    understanding
    the agony that destroyed
    You,

I too salute you,
    Because there must have been something
    truly great you had;

And if you ever get round to setting up
    another *house of truth* where you now are,
Be sure I'll be joining you over a *haja*
    one of these days –
    So long as it's not in heaven but some
    better place yet untouched by the
    foul hypocrisy of pious men.

Meantime I salute you,
    Drunken angel with golden wings:
Salute,
    Can *von* Themba.

I would mould a poem
    about you,
Only
  Words snap in the shaping
  Too brittle-coarse to take your form
    The mystic serenity of you;
So I am left with the memory of
  A lady giving alms –
    Vision of grace
      among beggars –
Inimitable you
    Giving alms.

JOE DE GRAFT *The Bean Garden*
[*To George A-W*]

Morning or evening,
Could mind cease from pondering
  Your words, George,
   As I pace my little garden
    Alive with spiralling beans
    New-posted in ranks of riotous green?
   Your simple words
   Spoken doubtless in spontaneous levity,
   But in imagination more terrifying
    Than towering *Ejuanema*
    Striding over-me-wards
    In five-furlong boots of virgin granite
    To pulverise,
    To annihilate kitten me:
*O God, we have pissed in your bean garden!*

My little garden
World planted with my ten fingers –
Spiralling heart tendrils: pride and hope . . .

'Twere a grave offence indeed, George,
Were it so;
For which we still devoutly believe
She would forgive us in her infinite love?
Delusion
To think there holds between us and God
An eternal covenant of malefaction and mercy.

*Odomankoma* forgive us –
  She who nurses within her flashing breast
  All the lightning of the heavens?
Woeful delusion

[25]

More terrifying
Than *Ejuanema's* earth-quaking footfall
Echoing down my kitten heart.

You'll come, won't you?
Come at seven and meet my wife –
   Plenty to drink
   And talk of good old days.

So we trooped in at seven expecting Sam
   Of old –
   Gay.

Come in, boys – and girls, right in:
   Small-dee and John and Ofori and Kobina
   And John's wife Mansa and Ofori's Elsie;
Here's Lou, my wife:
   We met in college – Columbia;
   She's a peach, ain't she?

And such a wife!
   Radiant as a Madison Avenue debutante,
   Shop-window legs and
   Swooning bust and, jeez,
   What a crown of dazzling hair!

Take it easy, folk, this is home.

So we relaxed.
   Lou shook us cocktails –
   East-coast mixtures richly blooming;
   Sam held her elbow and
     Afterwards
      Served the drinks.

[27]

We talked and drank
We drank and ate
  Dainty choppies.
The evening rolled on
  We rolled the floor away.
The highlife was good
  So was the jazz;
    And we danced
    To many tapes . . .

    While Lou killed us
      With sophistication.

Have some more,
      Won't you?
Bourbon?
     Try it – wonderful!
Soda?
    Oh no, best on the rocks!
Or would you rather this *and* that
  *or* that
    *or* that
      *or* that
        *or* that?

Oh yes, do try a bit of that, it's good!
  Straight from the States –
    Friends of ours, you know,
      Embassy, you know,
        Simply good, man, good!

Sam sat and drank
  Spoke little
  Gazed through the window
  While Lou sparkled.

  And we –
  We danced many a highlife
  Which we –
  We chased home with many a highball.

But Sam sat and drank
  Spoke little.
Marriage had come like a castrating angel flashing
  A platinum sword;
And Sam was subdued.

  We left them at the door
  Holding hands,
  His gaze at the receding stars,
  The early moon had set.

He will go in and clean up our mess –
  Mess left behind by
  Rowdy ghosts
  Conjured up from a youthful past
    By an unwitting invitation.

And they will retire.
  And tomorrow
  After the thousandth mating session
    In fifteen years –
She all antiseptically prepared

  [29]

And he hermetically sealed up in durex
    (under duresse) —
  Sam will wake up no whit nearer
  His dream of a bouncing piccaninny,
    And lap up his milk and honey
    Presented on the dot
    In choicest transatlantic china-ware.

And since his leave is still office fresh
  He'll curl up in the settee
  And read his Time Magazine just
    delivered from the States,
  Daring no venture into the tempting
    world of his kinswomen
    (Black whores!)
  An aged man in his middle prime.

Oh Sam, our Sam,
  Tell us, old Sam
  (or whisper if you will):
    Where the gaiety
    The old rumbustious gaiety?
    Where did you shed yourself?

  Dare we ask her
  Dare we, Sam,
  Dare we ask your platinum wife
    From New Orleans?

Under the eaves of the filling station
    A lunatic escaped from the asylum snores gently,
    Double-bent in sleep like a broken lobster;
Two prostitutes drift homeward,
    Misty with fatigue
    Musky with many males;
A tattered watchman on his rounds,
    His smoky lantern swaying,
    Returns to his dew-sodden mattress
    In the shadow of the warehouse:
        Humanity lives on, thankfully free
            Though demented and broken
            Forsaken, exploited and sleepless;
        And I walk on in this very early dawn.


As I come to the front of the old fort –
    Once its steaming, smelly dungeons
    The last habitation this side of the world
    For slaves
    (Those barbaric days of long ago!) –
Three black prison vans arrive
Sweating with dew from their night journey
        From the heart of the country
        To this – their unknown destination.
Slowly, smoothly,
    Like a well-tended engine of torture
    In its first unhurried stirrings,
The black gates of the fort swing open;
Muffled guard voices give the okay
The sweating vans move forward inexorably –
        One, next, then next –
    [31]

And vanish into the gaping gateway,
Merging with the blackness within.
The gates swing shut.


But I have seen them,
I have seen the men huddled within the vans,
    Unmistakable;
And I know that they are doomed,
By the odour I know:
    Odour of mildewed maize-cobs
        That farmers heap away in damp corners
        To await the regular ritual of the morning pit!
O God, how could love of fellow-men undo so many?


I slip round to the back of the fort:
    There stands an ancient rock.
The waves roll in, crested as with foaming hate,
    They roll in from the sea
    Rear up menacing
    Break against the Rock
        With a boom and a splash of spray
        Bubbling furiously;
But steady the Rock,
Steady.


This cannot be our last farewell to them,
These men who sought life's justification
    In their battling against injustice;
The cause of Freedom and of Justice is not lost;

The sea destroys
    The sea unknowing also builds.
        Salt of the sea, preserve them;
        Spray from the sea, shower on them grace;
        Rock ancient as time
          Give them of your strength.

O! for the hands
and the listening ear!
  The hushed throb of the drums –
  rhythming in pent-up labour –
  awaits the drummer's hands.

The drums' mute vellum, though unplayed,
is even now pulsating.
Mute but heard!

Where's Agama, the ace drummer?

Tall however be a road, it will not climb a tree.
How come the drummer's journey's ended in a tree!

Is not
the doorstep
ever the journey's end?

Call forth new drummers, for,
assembled in the village close,
the youth will dance today.
Agama's left the drum;
call forth new drummers, call;
for, dancing feet will dance today!

CHORUS:  The streams are full;
         why not the pots on mothers' fires?
         O! for the hands and the ears
         and the rhythm of the drums;
         and the home fires burning
         when the pots are full!

Dread Nagasaki
  stay your hand a while
    a while

Spare the architects
  of fire a while
    yet a while

Skyward we build
  gangdom's underworld
    of techno-
      logia.

Upward we build
  a marvel for our god:
    a syndicate of crime and hate.

Peace on earth, goodwill to men!

A thousand millennium more
The grasp beyond our reach.

The 'love' and 'peace' by which we swear
Are threadbare with abuse
As freedom and equality,
Democracy and the like.

Donning 'peace' as hood and mask
We mount the booster rockets now;
And love's the nose cone of the megaton load.

In Mars and in the Moon, maybe,
Some day, the reach our grasp!

There! Upside down, and standing on their heads!
Tumble-down woods in a tumble-down world.

The sun was still in bed; the wind asleep;
and slumb'rous sprawled the lake,
so calm and yet so treacherous.
There, like a belly-full python with room for more,
the lake surveys the world of men; – herself
the mirror of the world that lives by her.
In it the tumble-down world of trees and hills
and the sky, living double here and there.
The blades of grass so still.
Palm and bamboo leaves so staid!
No waft of wind disturbs the flood.
Not a ripple, not a shimmer.
All, all calm.
The tumble-down woods so still!

From the stillness and the hush,
from the depths of the lake,
come voices none can hear,
but all, all comprehend.

Away!
They tell me Song is dead,
   and those who sing today
   are those who're hungry
Mouth that's full has other jobs than sing.
And mouths are full –
   Our mouths.

D'you tell me: all there was
   to say about the pretty little rain drop
   that travelled all the way to earth: –
About the solo tree that stood
   a watch a-top the line of hills –
   all there's there to say was said?

'And all there is to see!' they said.

And I need must no more
   my childhood steps retrace,
   when fires swept the plains
   replacing soot and ash
   for frisking rabbits, mice
   and fluttering leaves!

We bruised our knees, and burnt
   our soles in smouldering ash;
   our skins were smeared as dark
   as piccaninnies of the slavers' South;
Nor cared, so dusky dark!

G. ADALI-MORTTY

Nor father, mother, anxious, traced
  us sons, though far into
  the wilderness we roved.
They knew!

They knew that kids must play
  and pulsing hearts must sing.
In freedom, free, they let us probe
  the burnt-out fields – our hunting ground.
They knew that kids must play.

Last night, cold winter's gale its worst
  on roads and streets, from gorge
  to tower did wreak its worst;
And I, in clumsy snow boots,
  the warmth of Nana, Kodzo, came to share.

They brought the news. They said it short
  and crisp, as though it were
  white snow flakes falling on the cheek.
They said, – nor cared they
  the wrench it plied: –

They said: the boy who knew
  what's childhood's play,
  who loved the rabbits and
  the mice, and the flapping leaves, –
Who, too, was left in freedom
  the fields to search
  where searing flames had swept
  to ash and cinders, smouldering, all
  that's life, like flies and crickets, and under-brush:

[39]

bush paths of lilting antelopes and duikers, –
their cold and watery noses quivering fears and doubts,
and messed up by ash and fallen, char-black stems; –

They said: 'He died the other day.'
He died who knew too many kids
   had died, who knew, though mouths
   are full and songs were drowned
   that little kids must play,
   and song's not dead.

Mistletoes of thought
with falsely tender
matchstick flowers
prey upon the mind
where cloud flowers –
sunset-flushed –
should grow instead!
O! for the wings of a mountain bird
that from the thoughts
I high and away may soar!

Or, for the scalpel's neat removing edge!

Instead
to plant a garden of the sky
with moons and stars
and fluttering wings of every hue.
Orchestrated woodlands, whose
virtuosos: song birds,
and leaves in the wind,
and heaving, swelling, eddying waves
like waves in deep mid-ocean!

Untutored harmonies,
and jasmine fragrance in the air.
Overhead – the rhythm of moons in orbit.

[41]

You may excel
in knowledge of their tongue,
and universal ties may bind you close to them;
but what they say, and how they feel –
the subtler details of their meaning,
thinking, feeling, reaching –
these are closed to you and me forever more;
as are, indeed, the interleaves of speech
– our speech – which fall on them
no more than were they dead leaves
in dust-dry harmattan,
although, for years, they've lived
and counted all there is to count
in our midst!

Now, we are old!
We too once climbed the rising slope
with eager youthful feet.
Now, stand we upon the hill's crest.
Here, we take our place
at the brink of another day.

We sowed the grain; we reaped.
The grain, ungathered, which grain-eating birds
have spared, together with the roots we left
unhoed, will sprout their good and bad to bless
and curse the later tillers of the land.

Those youthful feet, so light,
take up our place below in the bowl;
and up, and up they come,
so light of feet,
to take our place at the brink!

Old suns set;
new suns rise
on the mountain top,
as always suns have done,
and always suns will do,
till fizzle time
when all is spent
and all disintegrate
like glass on impact
into crystal bits;
or else erupt –
volcanic lava flowing without a bed!

Tell them who climb the slope,
we saw the first suns rise;
the first suns set!

Our voices flow with the waters
down in the bowl below
where young feet take our place.

Aroma
from the pots of three busy mothers
  in the dusking trees
    floated over the forest air
binding the sharp desires of twenty kiddies

    Laxing ancient sinews
      dreaming still
      of their labours
      past
        and to come

Eyes transfixed on the bowl in the sky
  lying high
    above the towers of foliage

The infant moon
  the bowl
    when begging East
is said to be a lucky month for the tribe

    Eyes transfixed in hope
hearing yet unseeing
    while the last bird hurries by in flight
      to its mountain perch
        on the skyey twig
          of the sacred odum tree.

    The dusking evening
veiling the restless hands
    and tireless feet
      of mothers three

[45]

abusy with the only soup
of the day
while the laxing limbs
of Dad and his associate mortgaged men
and gun-initiate brothers
twitch
in restless dreaming –
of the farm and falling trees and
wailing fauns
drowned by the eery chorus of night
and that in turn
swallowed up afresh
by the jungle

In the distance
the roaring tumult of the flood and the
gurgling waters
hurrying down to sea.

I

Goat shit on gutted alley-ways
and near-rooted huts of mud
their peeling thatch a plaything for the termites

  fluting dwellers of the woods
and muling herds their throats interleave
through the shadows of the night

  countless peering eyes crowd
the village in
    seeing but unseen
and the sky lamps pierce through
the night winds that kill
earth mother's reed candles –
    the sky lamps
    the tougher of the two
    but hardly brighter

II

Through the cracks in the walls
the baby talk of learning hands
training on the drums
the master drummers tuned

  while the nailless toes
of master drummers grope their way
into the fumes of sleep

[47]

spare of flesh and no excess
of paunch to fill
they go to sleep content

tomorrow
leathery palms and fingers shaped
by use like pincers sure must close
on hoe and cutlass handles

spine bent double
on the cutlass fit as day succeeds
the night

III

The dim embers
on the faggots' heads
glow their mysteries
in the dim huts of sleep
    and drowsy eyes
salt-wet with smoke
shut
to multiply the mist-eeries of dreams
brought forward from the day

Dad mams and kids all sleep
on floor mats
while the sky lamps
peep and keep the watch
through the star holes in the roof

IV

Through the fumes of sleep
are heard the taps in the palm raft door
as the early callcocks' crowing
disembowels the dew-gemmed dawn

   other shuffling soles of village wives
are heard
their way to the valley watershed trudging

   for
mothers' absence
from councils at the Elder's court
is felt as presence
mellowing deliberations of the men

   where
heads meet heads
to patch the rifts of wrongs

Fearsome and dark are village nights!
How odd of me
To near-forget those village nights.
Here, seen through baccy smoke
The spectred looming gloom
Here, in Aloka, harrowed by the hush,
Reminds me.

The only voice a cricket's
Chirp-chirping from the rice that's wet, so wet,
Standing all its life in swamp.
Village nights are not like city nights so bright,
So companioned and so safe from haunting gnomes.
Village nights are different.
Dark, so dark and dank.
I'd half-forgot the pitch, the blinding pitch
Of nights of childhood and of youth.
As man I thought 'twas fancy
Made me fear the darkness
Of the nights at Gbogame
The village of my birth.

There, behind each hillock, tree or bush,
Stalk imaginables various,
Whining, groaning, moaning, sighing;
Nymphs, goblins, arrow-carrying dwarfs
In every wood. They vied with us
Collecting berries. They envied
Us, the children of humans.
They spoilt our play, and licked our soup.

Where are they, the spirits of the night?
Where? Here, Aloka nights repeat
The nights my village knew:
My childhood's nights so dark!

When I was very small indeed,
   and Joe and Fred were six-year giants,
My father, they and I with soil
   did mix farm-yard manure.
In this we planted coco-nuts,
   naming them by brothers' names.
The palms grew faster far than I;
   and soon ere I could grow a Man,
They, flowering, reached their goal!
Like the ear-rings that my sisters wore
   came the tender golden flowers.
I watched them grow from gold to green
   then nuts as large as Tata's head.
I craved for the milk I knew they bore.
I listened to the whispering leaves:
To the chattering, rattling, whispering leaves,
When night winds did wake.

They haunt me still in work and play:
Those whispering leaves behind the slit
On the cabin wall of childhood's dreaming and becoming.

And the joy of the homecoming
with the clansmen's ribald welcome
Hand-shake, hug and *woe zɔ*!
*woe zɔ*!
ringing all around

And old Ma's pride
unbowed
bringing in the rear
Though in body
fragile
decrepit
hobble-de-hob
unbowed in spirit yet
old Ma's pride's unbowed
She brings the rear
in the full blossom of achievement

She comes
her son –
the coming man –
to hold onto her breast
– with luck to lift him off the ground
as once she did
and on her cosy back to wrap him up again

In the trees
  April winds!

Through the window
  Thoughts like April winds:

Foregetmenots
  And birds protesting the setting sun.

What's there to show
  For living and desiring?

The open book on the lap
  Like April night
Closes,
  Sudden, Total.

The winds and the voice of children at play
  Will join the song of birds

Tomorrow,
  Though women wail,
And castles crumble in the sand.

Silk-cotton floating, weightless, down,
Lies about, how heavy
Whatever angry heavens
Cast down upon us is:
So heavy, it can drown
A crew entire in any
Ocean-liner with its surgeons
Lifeboats, hosts, cargo, pleasure domes and compasses.

A marked Jacob limping home
Drumming his arrival with a stick
On the stony road
Brings news of struggle
And a crowded ladder;
Of a temple land mark
At a concrete place
Where man may stretch
Himself to match his fate
In prayer, in struggle and in dream.

The place of struggle
And the place of fire
Share one divinity.

There man is met,
Addressed by destiny,
Made stronger and refreshed.

And what he takes away
Is not himself or of himself,
But from, and of another.

The place of fire and of dream
Saw the old tree
Of our lives blown down
Rotting and returning to the earth
That gave it life:
In its place
Is a green flame in bright light,
Fertile, easy on the eye
Reading, in an act of prayer,

[56]

In adoration and delight,
Or meeting other eyes in love
Finding that the place of dream
And of the mystic burning bush
May lie close, here in a book
Or open in a lovers' look.

Torn strings of violin trail.
As the stage turns,
We move into light or into darkness.

In strong light, eyes ache, water, blink;
And blurred vision fogs the mind.
In darkness, we can only dream:
And our dream mocks
With ghosts of unrealities,
Or laughs white, wide and widens
Into threat.

But when we look beneath
The dreamy threat or the blinding light,
We see we move among friends and heirs:
Trees with seeds to grow
On our graves:
Trees which flower written notes
From deeper spreading roots saying
'High above, the air is free'
Or 'Fee of life is use of self'
Or 'Self is seed . . . and
In self is a shelf
Ready to the knowing hand'
Which, pulling it, makes it grow
Leading it and us into another world,
Another dawn with a feel of childhood in the air.

A bridge is thrown
Across a lone
Stream. To stand
The weight of a band
Of soldiers in full kit,
On both banks, it
Needed firm ground.
How sound,
My friend, is your side
Of the bank? Astride
Our worlds, we gape
At the rape and foul escape
Of poisoned thoughts
Drowning many of all sorts.
Can your bank, my friend
Hold a bridge at its other end?

We till the soil around the mango tree
Because we care for these:
For surface beauty of a youthful skin
When swelling, rounding fruits fill with juice;
For health of inner tissue and of seed.

Have you looked out up the night sky
At the moon eclipsed
In Africa, away from city lights,
And felt alone
Yet expanded in bright company
Holding in your very being
Stars, milky ways Universes
In a sky you form
With other beings of your kind?

Have you felt one in sadness
With a crowd beating bared doors?
Shared a shocked awakening
In foreign lands when freezing doubt
Splashed on your very beings
From hosts of hostile or avoiding eyes
Which made you feel out,
Yet made you want intensely to be in;
In, as originals,
Not faded carbon copies of another:
In, as Ghanaians
Nourished by the sounds, sights, tastes
Stimulations of home
Rooted in a home manure
Natural and rich
Till you grew proud branches in a Tropical
Sun – branches for eagles
With blood on their wings, flying home?

And when your voices link in chains
To show that you belong,
Does Odomankoma Drummer put

[61]

On you in verse, in proverbs,
A rich Kente heritage of what
You are and must aspire to,
Singing the familiar hymn

*'Amanson Tweduampon*
. . . . . . . . . . . . . . . . . .
*Nyame ma Ghana man ngyina*
*Nhyira nka no mu mba nyina?'*

If he does, let
Your shared shock spread a sky
Over you in a nation feeling
Reaching out for meaning
    In our present struggle for prosperity –
Our savings for posterity.

Against the darkly curtained dawn
Shadowy figures carrying nets
Raffia bags with the day's meal,
Paddles, calabashes, water,
Move swiftly to the beaches.
For cockcrow must see them out
Rowing into dawn, at sea.

We must also out and move
To where the day was calling us.

At the outskirts, fisher women
Light dry sticks with kerosene
In round herring-smoking ovens.

And pregnant sheep from sleep awaking
Slowly lift their burdened forms
And waddle safely out of way
Uncaring what our search was for.

Past a shrine, discarded dustbins
And the junk of life in boats
Came we to the River Prah
To a place of broken pots
Half burried ruins and of bones;
Human bones white with age
Teeth grinning from the mud
Gold rings on finger bones
Skulls, femurs, pelvic girdles
A settlement, or burial place?

A path behind a knotted grove
Took us to a sudden clearing
And right in front and either side
Rose the sides of towering mountains
Lines of rock, sculptural:
Looking like female forms
Bending over sacred secrets.

The sun parted shadow curtains
From the rising forms of rock
And in the rays the common rocks
Were line on line of gleeming ore
Waiting to be mined.

The high noon sun is dark;
Its light goes black:
We can no longer mark
The hawk's attack.

Stray senses touch sea waves
Receding, rimmed
With what a black world craves: –
A life unskimmed.

Deep Darkness drugs the sense
We do not need,
Till rising blackness sends
a light of seed

To germinate and leaf
Within each wall
Of selfhood and belief,
That will not fall.

Then blood, black blood and sap
Will lace the leaf
And send strong offsprings up
To lighten grief.

Falling leaves whirling upwards
Mirror rioting trees stampeding under fire.
Naked branches scratch the air,
cry, shriek, seeking shelter, signalling the sky.

Passerines pecking grains grip in vain
The iron railing leading to their food.
They jump ruffled down the slippery snow
Chest feathers fluttering!
The feathers smoothen in a sudden calm.

But ruder winds lash again
The tree tips into splashing waves
And one small bird
whirling dizzy
tells how it feels to be
A learner swimmer
caught under waves.

All that is left
Of the prophet and the book
Is paper filled with sand
For moral carpenters
Who do not need a church.

A. KAYPER MENSAH *Damirfa*
[*Old Africa* . . . .]

I stand by your grave,
Lift the stone that hit you
On your face, your temple and your spine.
*Damirfa due, Damirfa.*

My slander slashed your face,
Slashed your drum
Burnt your roof, broke your spear,
Plucked your plumes, left you ugly,
Bled you of your self respect,
Made you feel a foolish foul thing.

But now I know
I spoke too early and in error,
Sought to tell myself I'm different
Someone other, better far!
I looked not deep enough to see
That you were wet for lack of shelter;
That I am dry, flying over the clouds;
That for a man above the clouds,
It does not rain.

*Damirfa due, Damirfa.*

A. KAYPER MENSAH *Purged of Failures*

Sleepers in a nightmare
Rain on the shore
To be rolled out to sea
By the swift receding waves;
They lift themselves
In suffocating torment
Rugged and awkward
In their water-clothes
Drifting into sea
To face the fishes
And the judgement of salt.

Our student days
Are out at sea
Our failures, our fears;
And in my boat
Alone at sea
I hear no self-reproaching
Shameful eyes,
Only the lapping of the waters
The laughter eternal
Of smoothly moving waves,
The benediction of the friendly sands
Pearly in the watery light.

A thin dark curtain of one night
Is all there is between me and the
Foul horrors from the steaming rot
Of superstition and disease;
Below the fresh hygienic consciousness
Your world expects, but you reject –
You who have whole centuries
Of thick black blocks of concrete
Night between you and the horrors.

So seek some other would-be dancer
Who will dance your beat, and rock
To your anarchic morals
'Because I do not hope to turn'.

In the morning sunlight
I looked up at her.
Her face exactly an idea:
Neatness, softness, sweet experience
Overcame me, stretched my bow
Flung my arrow over fluttering sails
Of her hair moving in the waves!

And I who could not see her move
Without a feeling for a feast
Followed her to banquet halls.

A ship just in from Africa
Unloads at Tilbury docks
Brown pea-nuts and cocoa-beans
Timber and black men.

Another ship prepares to leave
And loads her goods and men.
Printed on the waiting cartons
Are familiar sentences
'Made in England – Cadbury Chocolates,
Refined Nut Oil, Furniture.'

But up the gangway climb nine blackmen
Bearing on their furrowed brows
'Niggers – Made in Whiteman's land'
They came to find an aim.

KOFI AWOONOR *A Dirge*
[*To be sung to slow drumbeats of ten-second intervals*]

Tell them tell it to them
That we the children of Ashiagbor's house
Went to hunt; when we returned,
Our guns were pointing to the earth,
We cannot say it; someone say it for us.
Our tears cannot fall,
We have no mouths to say it with.
We took the canoe, the canoe with sandload
They say the hippo cannot overturn
Our fathers, the hippo has overturned our canoe
   We come home
Our guns pointing to the earth.
Our mother, our dear mother
Where are our tears, where are our tears.
Give us mouth to say it, our mother.
We are on our knees to you
We are still on our knees.

Let all of you stop the death-cry
    and let me hear.
It is home; I stood at death's door
    and knocked throughout the night.
Have patience and I shall pay the debt.
Suppose I had someone
    Someone who will call me the dove
    and it will run and come to me.
I have something to say I want to say
    But it surpasses saying.
The dove says it is the soft voice
Which takes gifts from elders.
The prepared-for war is never surprised
So have patience
    and I will pay the debt.
I knocked at death's door all night.
It was only the sleeping crow who came.
Go back and prepare your gods
    and then come back
So I left; I am seeking to prepare my gods.
    I am seeking; I am seeking.

The sea-god has deserted the shore
And the day-land net lands with catches of weed
Then the storm came
Chastening the birth bowels and chords of sacraments.
We stood on the shore and watched you sail
To the roar of the sea and the priests bell.
They didn't forget to place the sacrificial cow
On the bow of the storm-experienced canoe
Anipaye the fish, I shall stay at the net's end
While you go down.
While you go down.

I shall be under the tree
And the rains will come and beat me
And the tree will die and leave its branches
And Anipaye you will go down.

Then you were lost where earth and sea met
And we didn't know what happened.
The sea roared and ran around
Like the mad man at moonrise.
But it stopped, it suddenly stopped.
The cow and Anipaye had gone down.

When our tears are dry on the shore
and the fishermen carry their nets home
and the seagulls return to bird island
and the laughter of the children recedes at night,
there shall still linger the communion we forged
the feast of oneness whose ritual we partook of.
There shall still be the eternal gateman
who will close the cemetery doors
and send the late mourners away.
It cannot be the music we heard that night
that still lingers in the chambers of memory.
It is the new chorus of our forgotten comrades
and the halleluyahs of our second selves.

feasts tortured smiles
after; the painful purgation
   and we sleep
   dreaming of purple paradises
   of laughter of naked virgins
in the arms of buffoons
fetid vomit
loud raucous music
rending the dream of skies
the smell of sacrifice
as the lord takes in
   the exhalations
and gathers unto himself
twelve baskets of feasted bread
   the lonely army
   lost in the city streets
Singing its last songs to sunfall

The joy, brothers, the joy!
   of waking up
   breathing the benediction
of yet another dawn.

The bowling cry through door posts
carrying boiling pots
ready for the feasters.
Kutsiami the benevolent boatman;
when I come to the river shore
please ferry me across
I do not have on my cloth-end
the price of your stewardship.

I do not know which god sent me,
to fall in the river
and fall in the fire.
These have failed.
I move into the gates
demanding which war it is;
which war it is?
the dwellers in the gates
answer us; we will let that war come
they whom we followed to come
sons of our own mothers and fathers
bearing upon our heads nothing
save the thunder that does roar
who knows when evil matters will come.

Open the gates!
It is Akpabli Horsu who sent me
Open the gates, my mother's children
and let me enter
our thunder initiates have run amok
and we sleep in the desert land
not moving our feet
we will sleep in the desert
guns in our hands we cannot fire
knives in our hands we cannot throw
the death of a man is not far away.

I will drink it; it is my god who gave it to me
I will drink this calabash
for it is god's gift to me
bachelor, never go too far
for the drummer boys will cook and let you eat.

[79]

Don't cry for me
my daughter, death called her
it is an offering of my heart
the ram has not come to stay
three days and it has gone
elders and chiefs whom will I trust
a snake has bitten my daughter
whom will I trust?
walk on gently; give me an offering
that I will give it to God
and he will be happy.

Uproot the yams you planted
for everything comes from God
it is an evil god who sent me
that all I have done
I bear the magic of the singer that has come
I have no paddle, my wish,
to push my boat into the river.

On time's lap sat simmering
burnt on lost heart's desires,
tasks fulfilled not fulfilled
through joys dying,
pain reborn in hearts
that felt they have forgotten
but not forgotten forever
sleeping ever last of all
with the down sloping of hopes lost
reborn everyday in the anguish
of a forgotten ecstasy
long known of long shores
stretching through childhood memories
    birds and hunting at grandfather's farm far away
    and squirrels hide in time's harvest.

I can go placing maggots on those fires
fanning the innerwards; I can sneak
along like the crawling beetles
Seeking through dust and dirt
the lonely miracle of redemption
I will sit by the roadside, breaking
the palm kernel, eating of the white
with the visiting mice
throwing the chaff to the easternly wind.
But will they let me go?
to nowhere where I can see
the sunlight fall on the green waters
and the ferrymen hurrying home
across with their heavy cargoes
of man flesh, child flesh and woman flesh
I sit where can I gather my thoughts
and ask what I have done so long
why could I not eat with elders
though my hands are washed clean in the salt river
Where they leave the paddles in the boat
to be carried by children of strangers.

Coming to that land that day
where sand strip covers childhood
and youth's memory; there was no storm
that did not speak to us
divining the end of our journey
promising that our palms shall prosper
and we shall not die by thirst
in the same land; where our fathers
lingered, ate from land and sea
drank the sweet waters of the ancient palms.

Will they let me go?
and pick the curing herbs behind fallen huts
to make our cure, their cure
marking the potsline
the lingering desire of every marksman
returning from futile hunt
beaten by desert rain and thistles
on his shoulder the limpid hare
and empty guns; will they let me go
to hoe my own fields, plant my own corn
   to wait for rain to come?
The sacrifice of years awaiting
unlit fires, who to knowledge
prepared the feast of the resurrection
On many rivers' shores moved
the benevolent band, awaiting
   that season

The dawn second cock
split by the ears of rumour
time to wash the new corn
ready for the grinders
lighting the family fire of flimsy twigs
Broom sweeping unto dunghill
Crimes that my fathers atoned for.
Someday, by some rivers!
We sang that song before
in the thousand seasons of good harvest
and full fish following our fathers foot prints
on the long shores, homegoers.

They heard the thousand thunders
from the great river's waves

as the road crossing snakes brood on rotten eggs
that our feet should move to make room
for an empty empty valley.

What happened with cries heard under trees
that many households are empty?
The powder house is fallen
So we cannot make war
For when the bulls are alive
could the cows perform weed.

Did they whisper to us the miracle of time
Telling us over the dark waters
Where we came from? Did they
Call us unto themselves
With the story of time and beginning?
We sat in the shadow of our ancient trees
While the waters of the land washed
Washed against our hearts,
    Cleansing, cleansing.
The purifier sat among us
In sack cloth and ashes,
Bearing on himself the burdens
of these people. He touched our
foreheads with the wine of sour corn
and sprinkled our feet
with the juice of the jacaranda
Whilst the baobab rained dew on our heads.
Comforter, where is your comforting
With all our woes and our sins.
We walked from the beginning
towards the land of sunset.
We were a band of malefactors
And saints.
The purifier walked in our shadow
bearing the fly-whisk of his ancestors
for his task is not finished.
We stumbled through the brier brine
Consoling, moved against the
passion of rest forever
The touch stone of our journey
was the silent prayers of the purifier.
Then they asked whether the harvest
should be gathered. Who sowed the crops?

[85]

We do not know; but the harvesters
We know them.
They that howl all night in the lanes
returning every night from funerals
officiating at a million wakes.
Comforter, where is your comfort?

Gather us, gather us unto yourself our fathers
that we bear the terror of this journey
through the briar we stumble
bearing the million crucifixes of time.
Save us the terror of our burden.
Cleanse us.
The desert trees howl with wind-blows
for the waters had dried.
The sand which tossed in eyes
that opened wide in nights darkness
and there was light
save the silent prayers of the purifier
As we bore the million crosses
across the vastness of time
Then they appeared, the owners of the land
Among them were the silent lovers
of nights' long harmattans; questioners
at the fathers' weary court.

The girls bearing the flowers of the desert
Cinnamon and yellow pollen of the palm
Swaying through the earth beaten path fingers pointed
singing songs we could not hear,
Tearing down the glories of a thousand shrines
  and dancing

[86]

Muddying the paved paths of the fathers
annointed, and the offering
they bore on the wooden plates
asking for the glory of the fathers' rebirth,
Their penance-prayer voicing
unto the fathers
Not asking for forgiveness.
We sat among the thistles of the desert
chewing the cactus freshened
by the tear-drops of long-ago.
Revelling howlers in time's garden
   entering the forbidden grounds
   stirring us from that deep to time
the bearers' head turned to sunset
trampling through desert sand
   sang a song we could not
   hear the music of
It was the season of dry wind.

We are the sons of the land
bearing the terror of this journey
Carrying the million crucifixes of time.

Then we arrived by the river Mono.
There we planted our bean plants
Not to wait for the season of rain

The shiny shingles washed white
glistening like the sacred ram
sacrifice awaiting; the dart of surf thrusts
into the sides of the glistening ram
the foam topping the crest of the ram
The drums beat that day and many days

[87]

and still beat for the deliverance
from the terror of the burden of that journey.

I am surprised, not angry.
I am amazed
That one who professes
Such tenderness,
Such understanding,
Such sensitivity,
Could hurt another so deeply
And still not see
That there is something
Very wrong.

I too understand
What it is
To want to remain
Absolutely free.
I have felt the fear
Of chains that bind
And anchors that hold
And people who cling
In loving dependence.

Before you came
This fear has kept me free
From all entanglement.
I floated lightly,
Attached myself to nothing
Allowed no one to hold me
Long enough to make me feel possessed.
Nevermore, I swore,
Would I be held and bruised;
Nevermore use myself to feed
Another's desire.

[89]

To hide myself,
The self that still yearned
To touch
And in turn be touched
With the love
Of whose possibility I despaired,
I erected another self
Around myself:
I made it hard and sheer,
Glittering and smooth
And ungraspable.

What if this self was also
Unloveable?
Weighing the heavy pain of the
    aftermath of love
Against its brief ecstasy
And knowing how naturally unfair
Even real love is
For a woman,
I knew it was the wisest thing
To stay a refugee
From bitter experience.

When you came to me
With your empathetic talk
You did not win me completely.
All you did was split me
Between the hatred of being used
And the desire to care.
But that was enough.
Stupidly I opened up, blindly hoping

We could love an ideal
Independent love.

Nature makes it impossible.
I will not go again
To give myself hacked up.
Go create your great works of art
For which you need this desperate freedom.
I shall not be the last
To try alone
That other kind of creation
Which you have thrust on me.

Do not torture your mind
Searching for justification
I need none.
Enjoy your freedom.
Leave me,
Go.

I am now too old to look back
The urgent future faces me
And cuts from my sight the end
That should inevitably come;
The task that has been assigned to me
Remains unfinished and almost insurmountable
Is it fear of the wasteland at my back
That keeps me looking ahead
Or the lame struggling will to do the work?
Am I past the middle of the river
And therefore must go on?

Whatever it is or is not
My heart still throbs
To the old tunes
And the simple things of life;
Things that lie within our reach
But bound up in the fitful yearning
For the stars
In the dark expansive dome above.

We have come to your shrine to worship –
We the sons of the land.
The naked cowherd has brought
The cows safely home,
And stands silent with the bamboo flute
Wiping the rain from his brow;
As the birds brood in their nests
Awaiting the dawn with unsung melodies;
The shadows crowd on the shores
Pressing their lips against the bosom of the sea ⎯
The peasants home from their labours
Sit by their log-fires
Telling tales of long ago.
Why should we the sons of the land
Plead unheeded before your shrine,
When our hearts are full of song
And our lips tremble with sadness
The little firefly vies with the star,
The log-fire with the sun
The water in the calabash
With the mighty Volta,
But we have come in tattered penury
Begging at the door of a Master.

I was talking to a girl at the well
When they came to tell me
The sun has fallen
On the leaves.
Behind the forest.
I picked up my gourd
And went my way!

At home,
Adoma was treading waist-beads,
For her red passion cloth.
One by one, she clicked
One by one, for the loved one.
My wife sat by herself
All alone,
Spinning and singing.

The storm shouted
And his brother lightning
Smote down the door!
There was none to stop them, then.
They followed, the evil ones
They followed,
Followed me
Like wiry hunting dogs
With the glaze of the burning bush
On the ridges of their tongues.

They came
Dry and keen-eyed
And told her
There will be decades of nights

Till one day
When the gods please
There will be
Day again.
Because,
The sun has fallen
On the leaves
Behind the forest
And the stars are coming down
In dust and ashes.

If this is the time
To master my heart
Do so!
Do so now!
As the clouds float
Home to their rain-drenched
Caverns behind the hills.

If this is the time
To master my heart,
Let me fall an easy victim
To the pleasures that you hold to my lips
When the duiker
Lingers along the pool to drink
And the ailing leopard
Turns its dry unbelieving snout away;
When the dew-drops dry
Unnoticed on the sinews of the leaf
And the soft-paddling duck
Webs its way
Through the subtle
Entanglement of weeds,
Along the river Prah.

O, I remember the songs
You sang that night,
And the whirl of raffia skirts;
The speechless pulsations of living bones.
Oh I remember the songs you sang
Recounting what has gone before
And what is ours beyond
The tracks of our thoughts and feet

KWESI BREW

You sang of beautiful women
(The kangaroo-jumps of their youthful breasts)
Flirting with sportive spirits
Red-eyed, with red-lips, hoary-red
With quaffing of frequent libations;
You sang of feasts and festivals;
The red blood-line across the necks
Of sacrificial sheep;
Of acceptance and refusal of gifts;
Of sacrifices offered and withheld;
Of good men and their lot;
Of good name and its loss; of the die cast
And the loading of the dice;
Why the barndog barked
At the moon as she sang
And why the mouse dropped the pearl-corn
From its teeth and stood forced-humble
With the soft light of fear in its eyes.

I saw a sheen of light
On the soft belly of the leaves
Dream-worn in the night
Bright as the light
Defending day from night
And palm-wine as clear
As the path of a spirit as water,
And her hair like the dark eyes of an eagle
Over the affairs of men.

And yet the river rolled on
And passed over rocks;
White sand in the bed

[97]

Bearing the burden of rotten wood
Twigs, grass – a flower – the breath
Of the soil and the bones of thousands
Who should have lived
To fight a war for this or that
And this or that a ruse
To deceive the mover of the move
And the mover of the move
Always moved by an uncertainty.

And yet to fight
And yet to conquer:
This was the badge we bore
On the pale texture of our hearts.
And yet to fight
And yet to conquer.
The sea-gulls blow
Like paper-pieces over the hard blue sea
And yet we live to conquer.
So we talked of wards
With their women
And they wept at the foot of the hills.

And the waters rolled on.
And what was old was new
And what was new never came to stay.
But to skim the gates of change;
Forever new; forever old and new;
Once-upon-a-time,
Never the same,
Always at last the same.
And her hair was dark and her pride undimmed

By the dusty struggles
Of strong men over her shadow
And yet the river rolled on.
And the river rolled on.

Her thighs slipped-slipped
Through the folds of her cloth
As always, once-upon-a-time.
But those who slept with her in those mud huts
(Arrows in their grips
And bows on their shoulders)
Have crawled away soft-bellied,
Into hollow chambers
Along the road;
Lined their walls
With smooth white stones;
Abandoned the shade
That sheltered their peace
And call that peace of mind
Now floating away with the clouds
As peace –
That passes understand

If this is the time
To master our hearts
Do so!
Do so now!

We have come to the cross-roads
And I must either leave or come with you.
I lingered over the choice
But in the darkness of my doubts
You lifted the lamp of love
And I saw in your face
The road that I should take.

I dreamt I saw an eye, a pretty eye,
In your hands,
Glittering, wet and sickening;
Like a dull onyx set in a crown of thorns,
I did not know you were dead
When you dropped it in my lap.
What horrors of human sacrifice
Have you seen, executioner?
What agonies of tortured men
Who sat through nights and nights of pain;
Tongue-tied by the wicked sappor;
Gazing at you with hot imploring eyes?
These white lilies tossed their little heads then
In the non-stepped ponds;
There was bouncing gaiety in the crisp chirping
Of the cricket in the undergrowth,
And as the surf-boats splintered the waves
I saw the rainbow in your eyes
And in the flash of your teeth;
As each crystal shone,
I saw sitting hand in hand with melancholy
A little sunny child
Playing at marbles with husks of fallen stars,
Horrors were your flowers then,
The bright red bougainvillaea.
They delighted you.
Why do you now weep
And offer me this little gift
Of a dull onyx set in a crown of thorns?

KWESI BREW *Ancestral Faces*

They sneaked into the limbo of time,
But could not muffle the gay jingling
Brass bells on the frothy necks
Of the sacrificial sheep
That limped and nodded after them
They could not hide the moss on the bald pate
Of their reverent heads,
And the gnarled barks of the wawa tree;
Nor the rust on the ancient state–swords,
Nor the skulls studded with grinning cowries
They could not silence the drums,
The fibre of their souls and ours –
The drums that whisper to us behind black sinewy hands
They gazed and
Sweeping like white locusts through the forests
Saw the same men, slightly wizened,
Shuffle their sandalled feet to the same rhythms.
They heard the same words of wisdom uttered
Between puffs of pale blue smoke
They saw us,
And said! They have not changed!

The past
Is but the cinders
Of the present;
The future
The smoke
That escaped
Into the cloud-bound sky.

Be gentle, be kind my beloved
For words become memories,
And memories tools
In the hands of jesters.
When wise men become silent,
It is because they have read
The palms of Christ
In the face of the Buddha.

So look not for wisdom
And guidance
In their speech, my beloved.
Let the same fire
Which chastened their tongues
Into silence,
Teach us – teach us!

The rain came down;
When you and I slept away
The night's burden of our passions,
Their new-found wisdom
In quick lightning flashes
Revealed the truth
That they had been
The slaves of fools.

The short days breathing
In sharp painful spurts
Die on the wings of the silk-cotton
Clouds homing passed
The unthatched roof of humanity.

The sleep-roaring dove
Shuts its golden eye-lids
Against the darkness of the night.

And still I sit here in the dust
Struggling to understand
The world and its words
And so I have sometimes cast
A hopeful glance over the shoulders of those
Whose hoes have helped
A friend to till a thorny ground
And wondered whether to look
In fear upon the past or to rejoice;
To rejoice that we have achieved so much
That so much has escaped
The eyes of the gods who hold
The rod of punishment;
That the red-clay kitchens
Of our ancestral homes still
Teem with the feasts of the year.

The song we sing shall be
Of our faith in humanity
And the upward surge of our hopes!
Like the waves we shall surge forward
And spray the tired faces of the gods
With the cool refreshing breakers of our spirits!

I have arrived at last, O my Lord
At your shrine;
The songs you asked me to sing
I have sung them all
On the desolate sands of my journey.

The morning dew filled
The chambers of my hair
And I felt the crown of your hand on my head.

I have arrived O my Lord at your shrine.
I have done the penance you ordered
But the peace you promised me stays
In your heart beyond my reach.

What you do expect me sing, I will not,
What you do not expect me croak, I will;
A bird sings what it likes without request.
I am getting old and have to look back:
It is a short time, it is a long time,
The idea is funny: it is my own time.
Some people have sometimes made me angry,
Some men have surely tried to make me sad,
Most men have quite often made me happy,
I have borne it all and I am grateful.
I have tried but failed to nurse ill-will
Because the matter and thought, are crippling.
One belated insight, though, I now have:
The flowers and shrubs in the garden,
You trim to let them have air, comfort and thrive;
You try hard to twist, bend, press or cut them
But those that cannot withstand the action
Quietly bleed, shrink, wither and die;
You sometimes forget they are so helpless,
It's a pity you have not yet found how
To deal with them so that in the end, you
Will not have to cry: 'It is all my fault!'

'Ut omnes unum sint',
The point is obtuse, I think,
That all men may be one!
The black and white keys won
Into harmony to settle
A matter man has scuttled.
The division is not there.
If you look everywhere,
No man is black or white;
I may be black but not quite:
My teeth are perhaps white, my skin somewhat dark,
Your skin somewhat white, your hair perhaps dark.
The trouble is in the mind,
It is not a matter of kind.
Creature comfort and security breed fear,
They cause the philosophy some hold dear.
Let everybody have them and man is naked;
The thinking and the psychology, too, will be naked.
And when everybody is naked, we shall all join
In a global dance forgetting the old facile motto.

They are happy because they shun worry;
They worry because they can't help it;
They look grand because it's theirs to seek trouble,
And in their excitement they have their pleasure,
And with their pleasure they unbalance nature,
And disturb those around with their unbalance,
And are never themselves when shocked into balance.

I sometimes never understand
What I think I understand,
And when faced with reality,
The scales fall off my eyes,
The tears trickle off my eyes,
My innocence has been robbed away.

But why should I not understand
Though cautiously I try first to understand?
Why should I have any worry at all
Though I do what I can to avoid it?
Should I blame myself or the universe?
Or is there nothing wrong but my verse?
Why is it what it is even if I am a fool?

The conflict, if any, is not with God.
I cannot have a quarrel with force
I have been trying much to understand.
It is, then, with the word and the servant.
Of the servant and the word, I prefer
The word to which, in freedom, I refer.

I know the servant has one large body,
But, like the hydra, it has many heads
Any of which may poison me to hell.
Unless, for safety, I follow the crowd.
Even if the servant has just one head,
I must be very careful how I tread.

I am, I know, quite simply a coward,
I have to have, I think, a march onward,
I blame myself, the word and the servant,
I cannot mock the word and the servant,
I'm not asking to be left on my own.
It's a quest to be nearer a force my own.

I who have sought God,
Have won the church.
I who have sought social justice,
Have won the glory of politics.
I have taken the bread
And missed the sweet honey;
I have tested honour
And missed the statue of happy remembrance.
The bees drove me off with natural authority
The marble, too clumsy to mould with magnanimity.

They were trees,
But they took the form
Of the animals
I loved;
And before my eyes had opened,
I had seen them multiply
Into thousands;
Soft skins
And strange scents,
Hinting at the mysteries
Of the deep forest,
Where raffia shoots
Do talk
And stones roll down valleys
Knocking tree after tree
Into a cannon's explosion;
What ho! Life is sweet!
Crabs under the pebbles
Of ice-cold streams;
Foam, scores of feet high
Rumbling poo-soo! poo-soo!
The river with red eyes!
And palm-wine not yet mature;
What a tree, the palm tree
Which gives nuts for soup,
Kernels for oil,
And leaves for thatch;
And when it's quite dead,
Sprouts mushrooms
Soft and round,
But we must carry
Water from the stream

[111]

Fast home;
So we accept the beatings
That follow
Our detected thefts.
Wheels oiled with okros,
Steering wheels carved
Out of boards;
Carriers pinched from
The tops of kerosene tins;
Oh Lord, which Ferrari
Can compete with this?
And one had to leave
This jasmin-scented
Fool's paradise behind
To face the reality
Of cold, technical, growth;
Where money is King
And every word
Has two meanings;
Where graphs and computers
Determine a man's worth
And naïve humanity
Is taken for madness;
But who can defeat Nature?
The dialectic of Life?
And so back
On my head
I walk;
In my long,
Warm dream;
Stopping only to ask
Whether it's really true,

As delectable
As the nipples
Of a maid
Just out of puberty.
Fish, freshly smoked,
One for a penny,
But where is a farthing?
Old cutlasses
Sold to the blacksmith
Bring cash;
And the schoolboy's pockets
Reek of fish,
Mangoes and oranges.
Birds!
What sweet colours!
Chocolate brown,
Golden brown,
Pink-white;
With green
And blue
And purple
Eyes. And voices
That sing songs
Of forest love.
And mouths
That are sweetened
By pawpaws
And nectar
From mountain streams.
Birds!
But where is a sling?
The Zabrama mobile shop

Has parked near the market;
A friend tries to buy scissors,
Distracting Awuni's attention;
I pretend I am looking
At the strips
Of rubber cut
From motor-car inner-tubes;
Here's a chance –
One goes
Into my pocket,
And – another again!
Now, here comes my friend
And we're off
After the singing birds.
Birds!
Awiraa Akua,
Little Emma,
Hankies sprinkled with perfume
And – the smell of sardines;
'I want you to kiss me
As you've never kissed before.'
'Why are you so strong?
You who look so frail?'
'Touch me, Darling,
Please touch me, quick!'
Birds!
What use would the world be
Unpopulated with birds.
So sweet, melodic and loving,
Alluring, tempting to the hunt?
We have no car
So let's make one;
To the carpenter's shed

We go
To help ourselves
To his wood;
We're often caught,
But we must carry
Water fast home;
So we accept
The beatings
That follow
Our detected thefts.
Car-wheels oiled with okra,
Steering wheels carved
Out of boards;
Carriers picked from
The tops of kerosene tins;
Oh Lord, which Ferrari
Can compete
With this motor-car?
And one had to leave
This jasmin-scented
Fool's paradise
Behind.
To face the reality
Of cold, technical
Imagination;
Which, dead as
Horse manure
(Since it can be taught
And acquired, ha! Ha!)
Rules millions of men
Who've never known Eden,
God, I'm grateful to you;
Oh God, I'm so grateful.

Vulture! Vulture!
Stinking creature
Who builds no nest
But nestles in the best
Of those you drive away,
What can you say
Now that the eagles,
Armed with talons
Sharper than needles,
Are throwing down lemons
To the beakless bees?
Will you dry up the seas
Because others bathe in them
You who never swam?
When that you'd seen water,
You'd thought fit
To flutter
Only your tail in it;
Or to fish in it;
But there are those
To whom a rose
Is more sacred
Than the putrid
Carcasses
For which you reserve your caresses.
Vulture! Vulture!
Stinking creature
Where are you now?
Stranded under the paps
Of a dried-up sow;
The dyspeptic taps
Of a muck-eater;

CAMERON DUODU

And you natter and natter,
Expecting the hungry bitch
To feed you rich . . .
Oh vulture,
Silly creature,
I would laugh at you,
Were it not so true
That – *I* made you.

Your infancy now a wall of memory
In harmattan the locusts filled the sky
Destroying the sweat put into the field
And restless seas shattered canoes
The fisher-folk put to sail by noon.

The impatience in your teens
Yet silent were your dreams
With the fires in your heart
Breaking the mask of innocence.

The evasive solitude in your womb
And the determination of your limbs
With eyes like the soaring eagle
Shattering the glass of ignorance.

Your infancy now a wall of memory
Before this you, like the worms,
Leaning on for vain indecorous dreams
And the cobras with venomous tongues
Licking the tepid blooms of hibiscus.

I want to remember the fallen palm
With whitening fluid of wine
Dripping from its hardened belly
In this forest of life.

I want to remember it from the road
With mud on my feet,
And thorn-scraped flesh
From the branches by the water.

I want to remember them well
The sight of the green-eyed forest
The jubilant voices of the frogs
And the pleading cries of the owls.

I want to walk among the palms
With their razor-edged leaves
Shadowing the yam and cassava shrubs
Under which the crab builds its castle
And the cocoa pods drooping like mothers
Breasts feeding a hungry child.

I want to remember them all
Before they die and turn to mud
When I have gone.

I am silent and you are silent too
The moment I disclose the truth to you,
You are much too proud and I
am but much more afraid, for I may rue
the anxious day I choose to show
My love for you. I search your eyes
That you shall break the silence now
and say, simply say it . . .
You lying creatures who make fool of men
Do your cruel tongues truly bleed
In speaking for once just the truth?
Now I disbelieve reality and lead
A life of lost sanity; accepting hate
As love, still for the truth I wait.

Be still, deep night.
Your turbulence arrests
My quiet heart,
And your ceaseless murmurings
Hum endlessly upon my driven stream
Where caged eyes forget to hide their dreams.

With the full-grown moon
Rise far beyond the distant stars
So your beauty'll skim like the arrow,
Or as a taut-string flies.
Yet shall I bid you sleep, deep night.

My sight will fade;
I'll no more surround your glades
With knowing winds.
And all this given right
Will bow before rejection.

And so, deep night,
Forswear my accustomed word.
The thunder heard will no more dismay;
With new perception than will day
Fade into you with no keen mystery
But soft persuasion.

These creatures of vanity!
What do they know
Of a single blazing star
In a pleading sky?
How can they feel
The exhilaration of tall brown spray
Reaching high to the bare cliff edge,
Bringing the kiss of a distant shore
To touch the cheek in gentle salutation?
Yet who are they to deny
A soul its chance to fly
And how dare they determine
Its degree of ecstasy?
In a world of indeterminate values
Even chocolate brown
Has its proportionate share
Of Aestheticism.

ELLIS AYITEY KOMEY *Farewell to Europe*

I have marvelled at your vaunt
When I landed at your shore
And have been aghast
At what you have in store.

I have roamed your streets
Narrowed by cobwebs of antiquity
And seen your feet that clamber about
With lust for false value.

I have felt your brothers die
Like sheep in your metal-jammed city
And watched your sisters too
Jump for no better than vanity.

I have heard you moan with no end
About your life and your weather
Raining when it should shine
And snowing well into March.

I have wiped your crocodile tears
When you started to cry
For the death of my sons
On the shores next to mine.

I have tried to understand yours
And compared it with mine
And before I leave
I'm happy to say . . .

. . . I'm going back
Back to tranquillity.

[123]

He rolled to me
His rolly-polly body,
A little white Mississippi boy.

'Up, up, up . . .!'
He pleaded,
With hands outstretched

His mother was
Quite taken aback,
Sitting by agape;
Onlooker.

I hoisted
That purity-in-innocence
Shoulder high,
Then lowered him
Face to face.

His face brimming
With smile and laughter,
And my eyes busy
Gathering dew.

I stopped deep
In Louisiana once,
A cop close at my heels:
What! *Go to the coloured side.*
*Don't sit here!*

Somewhat angry,
But indeed, hungry,
I could only say:
*Some day we will meet again,*
*Your heart changed*
*For friendship.*

I sat, though,
And was served soup
In a miracle-whip bottle
I still keep
For a keepsake.

Shadows have lengthened
And Kofi Ankonam, my friend,
Has taken to the long long road.

A rooster at sunset,
He has wandered home
With sleep
His only concern,
As if contented,
Henceforth,
Always to sleep.

Kofi Ankonam,
*Dammirifa due due!*

I have been a victim of chance.
Helpless, I watched
An idle timeserver
Leave me stranded
On the ticket
Of uncle inheritance.

I have been
A victim of indifference.
When once my father departed,
Custom cast me adrift;
But in my knapsack,
I carried
The tools of Faraday
To pry about my way.

I have seen
The smile of pain:
I have seen custom
Cut off my mother
With a shilling,
Once my father
Was no more.
I have seen custom
Cut her off
From the very cocoa farms
That calloused
Her sweet, soft palms;
My mother, cut off from
The very mains
That creased
Her youth and brow.

This robot called tribe,
Where is your head?
Where the dickens
Are your bloody guts!

Time
   an accomplice of waste
                is an image of expense
it is always spilling
        its angry hands
             wheeling
its consummate skill
          pounding
      like a drill on the brain
never to be stopped
          retrieved
       or
           replenished
forever whittling
        whittling
          whittling
        away
      away
    away
  away
away
  all the vast stores
        of
         being!

Drab humdrum and
Giddy halcyon birds
Tone his tune of nature:
Sh-h-hsh-h-h-h-hsh-h-h!
Quiet, please, less noise here!
Swaddling clothes of beauty
Censor freak streaks of moods
In man's moves,
Save for sterling deeds
And good turns.

Since eons, it's been
This order of no change,
Where growth and habitude
Are the mode of the day.
Boy, that
Surely salts it simply
Dreary, flat and jejune!

Wait! In comes the architect,
Quite a whale of
A hard-boiled midnighter.
With brazen accoutrements.
His bulldozer,
Oh, so-so long!
To shape shapes to shape
This whole earth!

KOJO GYINAYE KYEI *My Father Goes a-Hunting*
*Tonight*

My father goes a-hunting tonight.
Mother has stuffed his haversack
With mashed plantain, spiced with
Fish, pepper, onions, salt and beef
For his lone recluse in the
Deep night of snakes and scorpions
Of the jungle gloom.

My father goes a-hunting tonight.
And again, mother takes to
Her sour bed,
Worrying and praying
Wake-keeping for her man.

My father goes a-hunting tonight.
Sometimes his efforts are
Only a wild goose gaze.
Rain drops hit like bullets,
Drench him, cold and shivering,
Far away from human abode.

My father goes a-hunting tonight,
And the community is agog
Awaiting bush-meat;
Yet his only shot
For the whole night
Might turn out to be just
The reflection from
His hunting light in
The shiny, bright eyes
Of a rat!

[131]

The walls of my house
Have not been painted
For the past thirty years, or so,
That makes them stand out
Sufficiently prominently
In their dilapidated outlook
At our town centre.

A close look,
And a thick fat book
Unfurls page after page
In leaves of walls.

On these walls,
I wrote records of
My brother's missing sheep
And goats and names of girl friends
And births of cats,
Dogs and also tots,
Some of whom,
Today, can easily beat
The devil out of me.
Others placard my additions
And subtractions – many
Of them wrong,
In ranting scribbles of charcoal.

Oh, dreams of yesterday
Drifting by in relics
Of antiques, hopes
And the tears of childhood!

I had to use the
Charcoal and walls:
For white chalk was dear;
And for practices
And also to keep my
Square plywood slate
Virgin black velveteen
For good reading
After writing my bottom best
In the tests of the years
On those 'blue Mondays',
Long ago.

I don't know why
Lousy scribbles in charcoal,
Colouring my house
Dirtier and messier
Today, must walk back home
On real red carpet ways.

You wrested:
Wanderlust has flung me
Far to land's end.
Reason I gulp
The gall and wormwood
Of Kantamanto and Stout,
Face pulled taut,
In bitterness seeking relief.

Now even palm soup and palaba sauce
Don't taste right anymore.
Half-clad kids romp and jump
Before my insipid bemoaning stare:
That bonny music of crickets and things
Now is but a shriek to a shrill,
Relaying the rendezvous
Of missing rhapsody:
There does not seem to be
Any verve left in essence.

After good 3000 of knots and miles,
The talisman of hopes
Is my only tenure of strength!

Life – the only
Wayside inn
On this
Rough-and-tumble safari.
Every man jack
Of our party
Stops here overnight.
After that,
He is only
A memory.

Themselves,
Intrinsically,
Virgins of purity;
Over ourselves,
Little, little
Blobs of color
And shame!

We sat down there
By the hut-dotted valley
For one long week
Staring into the dry river bed,
Which lay there
Like a disembowelled prehistoric monster
With all its rocky entrails laid bare.
We sat down there and waited for the rain.

We sat down there
On the seventh day of the thirsty week
And waited and listened.

All was quiet,
The leaves had no strength to rustle.
The birds and beasts were too weak to utter a sound.
Meanwhile priests and priestesses
Before their altars and shrines
Raised up supplicating hands
To heaven and to the heavens.

We sat down there
Waiting for the rain,
Watching the tantalizing dark clouds
That had been enveloping the earth for days.

We sat down there
And waited
While birds and beasts and vermin
Deserted their uncouth habitations,
Heading towards the dry river bed
To wait for the rain.

We sat down there
Man and beast
With a single purpose –
To wait for the rain.

We waited, waited, waited
Until,
Suddenly,
Behold
The dry valley burst out in a watery uproar.
The leaves rustled,
Birds and beasts raised up their voices
In songs of praise,
And the sons of men
Raised up themselves
From their seats and knees
And walked back home
In silence,
And in thankful contemplation,
Strangely subdued.
They walked back home,
In silence.

There still was no rain
But there was roaring water
In the valley;
For God, they say,
Had been causing rain
Far far away.

He came unto me
Like the ghost of him
I killed a thousand years ago.
He stood behind me
In the ghastly half light of a moonlit night
And put his dead leaden hand on my shoulder.
He spoke
And his hollow echoing voice
Was like a sound which had travelled
A billion miles
To reach me.
He said, and the voice shook the air:
You have been escaping for too long
You have been playing
Hide and seek with me
In a maze
With which you are more familiar than I am.
I have sought you for too long.
But tell me:
Why must you cross, like this,
Your destiny and mine
Which has ordained
That you and I
Shall ever be together
Even beyond the end of time?
Ours is a timeless union,
Do you hear me?
Endless!
Come,
Come,
Come, follow me.
I shall make you immortal;

I shall put an end to the fear
That has haunted you for so long
And made you a fugitive.
Know,
Know that you murdered me
So that I may live.
I shall live beyond the end of time
And you shall ever be with me.
Come,
Come,
Come, follow me,
For the morning light
Peeps through the eastern clouds
And motions me
To my kingdom of glorious darkness.
Come, or forever
Remain a fugitive,
Forever frightened,
Forever haunted.

When the sun strikes hard the earth
And peeps into all dark corners,
When the sun strikes hard the earth
And creeps into all tiny chinks,
Then is the time to exorcize.

Remove him gently from his couch;

Dig deep his grave;
Dredge it deep
And clean and deep;
Then lay him back,
Very gently,
And drive a stake
Right through his heart;
Drive a stake
Right through his heart;
Then leave him there
Till judgement day.

How dare you imply or say
By those persistent questions
That I lie in everything I say.
But tell me, since when did you
Receive the news and how dare
You keep it all from me!
That's no matter – get up and
Let's be going – all this is idle.
How dare I come with your worship
Who am I that may come with you!
The dark cloud has just concealed the moon
And all is dark save for distant
Dim and blinking stars and
Occasional head-lights of cars
Dashing by, There was silence,
And the battle of silent feelings
Raged in our hearts.
The moon was just peering through
The clouds and I felt I had
Peered into the recesses of
Her heart, There was black hatred
Welling there, The clouds hid
The moon, A car dashed across;
Then it was all darkness.
Far away to the south
Red and Yellow lights gleamed
On the misty harbour.
Get up and let's be going
How dare I . . .
How dare you . . .
I held her hand and raised her up.
We must be going: We crawled

[142]

Along the road – to the door
Neither looking at the other all
The way, We looked straight ahead
At the lights on the misty harbour –
We needed lights, for there was
Darkness in our hearts.
Well, good night . . .
Good night . . .
And in the darkness of our hearts
You could still hear
How dare you . . .
How dare I . . .

I hid my voice under the sea
In an unknown land,
For my thoughts and lips were at war
With each other.
I had my body under the mournful cypress
For it was the battle ground for lips and thoughts.
And now that I am not
The two are at peace with the world.
Thanks be to God!

Sea boils
And the sun-parched skin is refreshed
And cool

Hen pecks
And Eve's chickens grin like
Happy children
At a wedding feast

Man smiles, and lo, the flash of flame has singed a soul.

I am not alone in the cold clutch of the world
In this dungeon of sightless bats, I'm not alone
There are true friends somewhere, I dream
Praying from hollows of man's brain
Imploring the spirit of dust
That in this hour of blank despair
The chains fall off my heavy heart
And all my feckless doubting cease

    There are true friends somewhere, I see
    Whose restless eyes are streaks of light
    I'm not alone in mankind's black night
    In the hopes of true friends, I'm not alone

When fellow brutes give bombs for bread
I will not be alone . . . our spirits shall find, nor
Inheritance nor peace, in domes of death

Condescension for compassion
I'm not alone . . . We have disdained the Word
Sack-cloth and ashes are still our proud lot

Bare daggers to extricate sight
I smile. I've trod that path before

    There are true friends somewhere, I know
    Whose pounding hearts are trumpet notes
    I am not alone in mankind's dark night
    In the deeds of true friends, I'm not alone

Self-righteousness is the strumpet of menial minds
If earth were full of naught but their arrogant gaze

Peering like angels that have crawled their way through
    hell
Then would I, unsighed, sigh. Then would I roam alone
The wall of Jericho shall not heed, stone for stone
    The trumpet's blare on either side
And I will shout, come crowded golden halls, come empty
    years,
    I have not stalked in vain.

My world pines in your marble breasts, daughter of woe
Green buds crack in the dry harmattan wind
Sun beats down on the city of a million dead
Men wove hats with their hands for a shelter
And monkeys, from tree-tops bare, mock
With crown-capped glee
Bare-headed among the despoiled flowers I stand
Empty-handed, in built-up deserts
I groan mankind's loss
And search wide heavens for a sign not written there

I am a stranger . . .

My mother's house is desolate and bare
I, stranger upon earth, walk alone the misty pavements
Where bright sun shines and brings no warmth
As snowflakes parachute to rescue earth

Yet you are shivering, daughter of the land

I feel, can touch and yearn to chant old psalms
Recorded on soundtracks through Adam's mind
But I am no more human
Purged of mankind-knowing griefs
Snobbery passes me by
And I have lost my voice
In the whining of the arctic winds bleak and sharp
Despair withdraws from my cold paw in friendship shot
Alone. I prowl, being with soul lone as a star
That twinkles in a firmament of crushed-out eyes
Depths are frozen wombs
Barren skulls and cross-bones picked
And earth belongs to other races – pressed in steel

I am lost . . . and you . . .
And what shall we make
Of all these shining orbs and incandescent tombs?

The sun is dark, is cold the sun
I am a potter's vessel shaped by knowing hands
Fallen from sky of earth-dreams that never flower
The eye of the Lord is on me
(and His wrath too)
How long,
How long shall I riddle rock breasts for warmth
How long shall I, a worn Silesian exile, turn
Sore feet for refuge to shrines of past oppression?

Suffer me
Oh suffer me not to be separated
Firm breasts that milked my toothless gum

In the desert place
Let my cry come unto Thee!

I shall return
I shall return to sun-warmed lands
Where rivers flow all through the year
I shall return with the glory of sun-down
Only to battered citadels will I return
To bashed-in skulls and sun-picked bones
Wild groans of shattered hearthstones pierce my ears
Knock, O knock down the battlements of pride

Caress stone breasts with benumbed hands
That fire may rise

[149]

And coldness burn
And warmth return
And in red glow, behold
That sign sure writ in blood
Shall these bones live?
Shall these bones live?

The streams of Life gush out in tuneful song
Dead bones in rocky caves astir
Dead bones in mansions moving,
As the glory of God descends on earth

To be despoiled.

Let us build new homesteads
New dreams to decorate these ruins
Let us weave fresh rafters from rescued stalks
Let us start all over again

The past is a pitiless dream
A dread nightmare, you may remember, which stared
Deep into our fearless eyes
We gave it glance for glance
Frown for frown
Fouler word for filthy word
And when it kept on staring
Like a senseless imbecile
We lost our minds completely
We braced ourselves to self-assertion
To knock this beast over
And so redeem our peace

And that, you may remember,
Was the storm clouds breaking over us
And death marching in
And flowering fields laid low
And children in the womb with them

Now we look back to the pity of the nightmare
Not being anywhere near at all
And to sad awakening that our stare
Had been nowhere but into blank brotherly eyes
Seized by delirium like ourselves
And that, had the black storm only given us
A moment's chance,
And not struck just then . . .
But the past is horrific reality.

How can I, who cannot control
My own waking and dreaming, ever hope to make my
    voice
    heard in the wrangling for mankind's soul?

How can I, dumb in my own self-defence
Dream of forging words of salvation for billions with their
    cares
    and well-drugged silence?

Madness is virtue's beholding redemption in pools of blood
    squashed from dreams and inexpressible fears of men
    whose sole bastion is the booth
(Which also is the paschal knife)

Sanity lies in submitting to the bitter-sweet dream
    created in factories of democracy by tired, drained-dry
    brains, doped to senselessness by fact-effacing ether
(Which is their sole refuge)

And I, blown by thick puffs of factory smoke
Mad neither for my sorrows nor the world's
Seek faith in the vision I know is false
In sanity I know is mere soul-effacement

And my doubts catch up with me in the flitting cloud
Which cannot provide an anchor
Which is as empty as a dream
And barren as the tomb

I, feeble, spineless speck, dare not hope by warm word
To wreck the sovereign peoples' dream
The salvation of the world lies in deserted garden –
In a blind worm's crawl.

They said:
Wherever you sit to chew tigernuts
It is tigernuts that you chew
It's the chewing
(And what it is we chew) that counts
Forget the scene. Reck not the time

They added:
No matter the colour of the object
To which we dab on black man's paint
The object will (try as it can
To fight against this law) take on
The colour of the clay

And then they mused:
The colour of clay is endeavour's mark
So striving will leave its mark
No matter how dark the hearth
Striving will gain its end
No matter where we live
Our teeth can chew the nuts
For the red clay of the earth
Can make the black spot red
And wherever we sit to chew tigernuts
We surely will chew nuts
Surely.

There is no point in looking around, I promise you
There is no point in staying around
The hour of hope is long, long lost
And I should damn well know.
Behind abysmal sea

> White shells grin murder
> Leprous lips lap pus
> Foam a-festering sore
> Sand without mirage
> Oases without trail
> Bells and no worship
> Voices with no sound
> Nothing left behind

Lift not up your eyes
Hills are hills no more
I turned to the sunrise
My distended senses
And it was all but mist
And the south was full
Of purple sunset
While west lay out of space

> There's no point looking around
> Salvation depends on beasts
> Still hear my parting knell
> There's no point looking back
> Just for a pillar of salt
> My loins are barren
> Like a thirsty land
> So there's no point in looking ahead . . .

The new-born babe asked with a gentle tear
'Where is my mother's breast?' And silence reigned.

In the last days
Strange sights shall visit earth
Sights that may turn to blood the moon
This sun to midnight – in the last days

But now, when swords are not yet ploughshares
And spears still spears
Harken you, my little ones
If walking, shaded by the mango tree
Or running naked, scorched by this blazing sun
You aught perceive
Now, while the arrow remains arrow
And the miracle of spears and pruning hooks
Still remains an unseen miracle
Remember my little ones
If perchance your infant feet do slide
And you find yourselves in some mysterious dungeon
Of black, vengeful Sasabonsam
In realms where dogs make speech
And horns adorn the human front
Where mermaids in their skirts of silvery scales
And chattering sea-beasts flout mankind
If in this strange, sub-human realm
Your eyes fall on a stone, a hard black stone
Lifeless and muddy, that has grown a beard
Pray children, pass silently by
Ask no questions
For you are face to face with the first days
And the beginning and the end are one
And in the end shall strange sights visit earth

Stones shall be turned to men
And men to stone

Sparrows beget eagles
And sand become good grain

So children
If perchance you see a hare that roars
Or an ape perched in a palanquin
Look on in silence. Quickly pass by
Quickly.

Woman with emerald swathed on your coppery flesh,
Yield, O yield like the rest,
Those orbs dancing
In the fold across your breast
Shall yield before your sun has set.

I am the snake that sucks
Sweet life out of eggs,
Yield she must yield.
In my eye is the curse
That must distress,
You must yield, O yield like the rest.

Love I the pillar of neck
Governing like a marvel the balance
Of load on your head
Yet must I break it –

Love I the shine of your skin
Yet must I dull it
With venom from my sting –

Love I the flaming melody of your frame
Yet must I silence it,
The ecstasy moving in your step
Yet must I make it burn out its fire
In me, a snake that must suck
Sweet life out of eggs,
I, that will not spare.
You smell of the woman Eve
And you must yield.

[158]

Come I then in the path you proudly walk,
Come I raging with madness of forest fire,
Come I, in the fever of my curse
Come I, to crush you,
Break the copper pillar of your neck,
Kill the mercury glint in you,
And leave you there
By the debris of your plantain load,
In the tangle of your emerald robe,
Spent, overcome.

She paused in her pace, and turned on me
A soul that speared my reptile frame
Until I writhed in a helpless coil
And the poison in me boiled
And clotted in the glare
From the splendour of her redeemed soul.

O woman swathed in emerald,
I am not able to be, as of old,
A cursed snake
And make you yield, O yield to me.

Her dark lips smiled,
Her dark eyes beamed delight,
The copper neck swerved back with its load,
And down the slope of the market road,
She strode.

The corn that vanished in the night
Was hope for a hungry man,
The rising sap so slyly drained,
His spent strength's refreshment.

    O thievery
  And what is a man to do?

If it's of man we speak
Then once upon a time is still our time;
There lived a man, a man who lives,

And he planted his labour in grain,
He rested his hope in trees of wine,
And his harvest was in sight
And his sap was soon to surge,

When wind-in-wing Sasabonsam
By hover-craft homing in
Self-in-jet-propelled,
Landed to plunder to the last grain
To the last drip of sap.

Devastation! Without a crumb
Without a dreg,
What is a man to do?
A man so doomed to hunger and thirst
Shall cry his doom on thievery overdone.

Feet-aflame Sasabonsam!
Did you never hear of him?
In his flesh was burnt the lesson,

    [160]

That thievery overdone
Provokes the over-dispossessed
To ignite a curse of fire:

For his deed in greed,
First his feet aflame,
Then his saturated hide aflare,
Then his head a shout of fire,
Then ignition in totality,
Then annihilation.

Since once upon a time is still our time,
A little to eat and a little to drink
Could still restrain a curse on the brink.

What else is there to say?

They came to capture and enrapture us with wine?
They have us on their hands in our drunkenness,
This is the crass carousal.

Oh, there will be turnover beyond all calculation,
Speculator and consumer coffers both consumed,
Zero for the reckoning then,
Worse! Ruination,
As we romp and crash
The cut-glass underfoot
Then romp upon the clutter,
Innocent of its value
Heedless of its pain,

It's your hearts will bleed, sirs,

It's you are unwined and capable of pain,
Our hearts are so anaesthetized,

You have us on your hands, sirs,
  As we devaluate value
    To impoverish us all.

Wickedness has fashioned a sword,
  Calls it a cross,
Bids us sacrifice to the sword
  Our love for the cross.

Our lips have kissed a Calvary cross,
  Could they lip the sword
Blood dripping from wounding, gutting,
  Paining God.

The weathered unjewelled cross
Wreathed with entrails of lamb dumbed
By orgying acolytes of the sword,
Whooping from their field of sacrilege

  If thou be the son of God
  Come down from the cross.

  My God, my God
  Why art Thou forsaken!

  And behold

There is a great earthquake.
The field of sacrilege is void,
Lightning melts the sword,
Showers wash the cross,
And the basic earth drinks in
The life-giving stream.

Then Easter flowers new born
As at the first dawn

Spread their vestment
Over the sanctity of Calvary

I see heads uplifting sprays
Give petalled gifts to the cross,
I see new lambs frisking up to Calvary,
And hear the Shepherd's live piping in the valley

To which I forever sing,
I will not sacrifice to the sword
My love for the cross,
Not wield a tyrant sword,
Not wield a killing sword,
Bear none but a Calvary cross

    The needy's cross
    The lamb's cross
    The life giving
      Blossoming
        Cross.

Night is the time when phantoms play,
   Flows the river,
   Phantoms white
   Phantoms black
Fish in the dark salt water bay.

Skulls are nets for phantom fishers,
   Flows the river,
Phantoms red on a phantom river
   Dark flows the river

Black phantom splashes
   Flows the river
White phantom splashes
   Flows the river.

Night is the time when phantoms play,
   Heads are nets
   For phantom fishers
There on the dark salt water bay.

   Phantoms black
   Phantoms red
   Phantoms white
   For nets their heads
And the dark, dark, dark river flows.

O empty space of farewell!
Where is touch,
Where is flesh-with-soul-beat?

Child stretching on a river bank
For mother-and-father's hand,
Where is touch to firm your faith
That life is warm and willing
To spare your heart a chilling?

Child who didn't make the river
Child who didn't give it temper;
Though its raging is real
You reach your hand
For flesh that is sailing farewell.

Don't cry baby,
Son, at two years old
You'll be a prodigy beggar kid,
Cute wide-eyed toddler beggar
Outside United Nations;
On that swanky beat,
'Painy-painy' lisping
And thriving on the coming in
And going out of world distresses,
Don't cry baby.

EFUA SUTHERLAND *Our Songs are About It*

Our songs are about It, and we are singers of life-driven
      songs,
We incantate,
We are too ecstatic of soul, too whole to lack laughter,
Gut-born laughter denuding It, wind-flinging It,
It has had to shed Its flags
Leave them dance-draggled in our dusts.

    Masked – marauder,
    Pilferer-of-souls,
    It comes to perch
    For dominance,
    Beaming benevolence.

Our songs are about It, we are singing still about It,
Our life-driven songs
We orchestrate,
We are too keyed in possession to lack laughter,
Lilted laughter that now from our dancing ground
Is tracing cadences throughout the universe.

    Earth, Sky, Water,
    Life, Death, Life Eternal,
    Our laughter pursues It,
    Ever and ever
    Our songs will be about It.

EFUA SUTHERLAND *Observation on a Cockerel About
to Crow, for a Young Man*

He's got a crow in his throat,
This cockerel,
Tick-tock, tick tock.

Give him a little time,
This cockerel,
Tick-tock, tic tock.
Neck constricted
Feathers huffed
Strained stance,
Defiance
Utterance inarticulate,

Watch that snigger, O spectator,

Soon he will boast,
This cockerel,
Tick-tock, tick-tock,
Of a real cocko-ri-koo!

Give him a little time,
This cockerel,
Tick-tock, tick-tock.

Male – fertilizers merely;
Female – incubators only;
Drones in pollination,
Spivs and butterflies bleeding the nation.
And neither Fatherhood
Nor Motherhood
The Vision
Or Mission
Of Poet
Or Prophet
Has meaning
Or healing
For those who sit in darkness
In the Afric wilderness.
Simony
Our Destiny?
Does Christ in the wilderness
Evoke the nothingness
Of dream or reverie,
An opiate of opium, dull and heavy?
Increase and multiply!
But to what end? – To die
For corruption
Or salvation?
And Schweitzer's proselytising zeal
To feed the poor, the sick to heal,
Will it in nothingness expire
To stress 'this sorry scheme of things entire'?
Shall these unselfish hands stretch out in vain
Across the desert land to sprinkle rain?

## I

When I am old
And lost my teeth
In service of the fold,
I shall go down without a wreath
Into my grave:
I shall go down
To music from a stave
Or two, and be forgotten by sundown.

## II

What matter then,
If the clock hand
Points to midnight or to ten
When I shall join in death's slow saraband?
If in the end
All shall be one
With atom and defend
No rights, what matters all the fields we've won?

## III

When I am old
And stale like bread
That lies for weeks unsold,
My children shall prefer me dead;
Will not believe
My innocence
Of protracting my leave
Or outstaying my welcome and my sense.

I told her what the Buddha taught:
She looked the picture of lynx;
I weighed what is against what ought:
She sat inscrutable – a sphinx;
I strained Tchaikovsky's tragic heart:
She smiled as if I'd made a joke;
And neither verse nor plastic art
Could sympathy from her evoke.
But when I bought the latest car,
I saw a twinkle in her eye
Like that strange light caught in the bar;
And then I knew her tongue was dry,
As parched as was her bedouin heart:
So to the nearest club we went –
The lost's symposium and the mart
For public gossipers – intent
To cheat that blind Old Maid before her shears
Cut short out span! The urge in her
Transcends my twilight life that hears
The Love-bird's call, but dares not stir,
Lest it should lose the dream of Eden
For the seductive snake's nightmare!
In this her element, sodden,
The gift of tongues descends on her:
'Oh! for a "frigidaire"', she wildly cries,
'That would express the brightest vision
Of the connoisseur, a lover worldly-wise,
Who boasts a "Jaguar" and a safe pension,
That cancer-scare cannot cut down the fags
He smokes, a man who dies but once, and not
Before he's worn contemptuously to rags
Life's motley garment, while his blood is hot.

O for a "been-to", neither old nor cold,
Whose purse is heavy – as his head is light;
O for some flotsam straw to which to hold,
Lest I should drown my beauty in the night.'

## I

Voices from the Void
Echoing Jung or Freud
Project distorted images
From History's unedited pages
On invalid screens;
Redeeming the pattern of genes,
They whisper a hint of fate,
Chorus to us too late
The movement of drama
From irony to tragedy or trauma!

## II

Doctrines of pundits
Buried under pyramids
Of social convention
Or mystical inversion,
Images tabooed or hidden,
Cravings repressed and forgotten,
Lead us an endopsychic dance from the dawning
Of conscience through stages of becoming
To individuation and non-being.

## III

Revere the ashes of outmoded culture!
But, remember, the starved vulture
Is a stranger to fame or shame,
Has minted no symbol or name
In its ordinary

And spare vocabulary
For mental illusion,
Lacks refineries of diction!

To My Future Child

### I

What ails my darling child?
Must you grow sour or wild
Because your pretty toy
Which was before a joy
Now lies in pieces on the floor
And is an endless joy no more?

### II

These tears you shed like rain
Are shed, my love, in vain:
For other toys, alas,
Will break this priceless vase,
Your heart, after this rainbow age
You pass, to turn life's chequered page!

### III

Oh, do not cry, my sweet:
For, other toys shall greet
Your heart with joy today
And those in time give way
To those that break the heart as soon:
Ah, do not cry for the cold moon!

### IV

I too have cried before
For pieces on the floor;

But now I cry no more
For toys not worth a straw;
I'll buy you yet another toy;
But treat it as a passing joy.

# BIOGRAPHICAL NOTES

JOE DE GRAFT, a playwright and initiator of the Drama programme at the School of Music and Drama, has published a play *Sons and Daughters* (Oxford University Press 1963). His other works include *Visitor from the Past.* He now works for UNESCO in Kenya.

He says of himself:

'I like to eat tasty Chinese and Mexican food when I can get it to eat, even though I have never been to China or Mexico; and I prefer the smell and tang of garlic to that of stinking fish, which most Ghanaians simply adore but which I detest. I love to read any author, no matter what his nationality, so long as I think he has something interesting to say to me (which means, if even in translation). High-life is my favourite light music; but I enjoy Mozart and Louis Armstrong and The Seekers no less than I do the singing of *adenkum* troupes from my home-town; just as, even though I am not a Christian, I find the language of certain parts of the Authorized English Bible no less moving than a well-turned Akan funeral dirge. And so on . . .

' "A welter of influences", you say; "a veritable whirlpool of cross-currents!" And I say: "So must I go and die?"

'But I prefer to answer in the imagery of fire: my imaginative life is like a fire that feeds on more than charcoal: butane gas, electricity, palm-oil, petrol as well as dry cow-dung and faggots have all kept it burning.

'I do not imagine that anyone of my readers will like more than a very few of my poems in this collection. These readers will have every right to damn me for writing such trite and "bad" poetry, if they so think. But I hope they will desist from asking me why I have not written them "African poetry". Simply because I am this individual;

[179]

neither a tribe living in some long inaccessible African jungle, nor a committee of pan-Africanist ethnographers.'

G. ADALI-MORTTY was born in Northern Eweland in the former British mandated Togoland which is now part of Ghana. Educated at Achimota and Cornell University, Geormbeeyi has had a very exciting career as a teacher, a social worker, adult educationalist and administrator. Until 1968 he was Ghana's Special Commissioner for Redeployment of labour. He started writing poetry many years ago, and may be described as the leading figure among Ghana's elder poets.

Geormbeeyi's poetry reflects his village birthplace of Gbogame. There are the sounds, the smells, the planting and harvesting of rice, which mark the deep attachment to his mother and to his birthplace. Though fiercely traditional in his material, Geormbeeyi has travelled widely – Brazil, Europe, Ceylon, United States. This is reflected in that aspect of his poetry that deals with far-away places, and reinforces his nostalgia for the undying values and the charm of his native homeland. Romantic and realistic at the same time, Adali-Mortty possesses a genius for grappling with the harsh realities and problems of modern African life and a remarkable ability to capture and sing about the ageing, alas the vanishing, Africa.

These scenes, and the world, possessed by shadows and fairies and creatures that shared life with man, as he says haunt me still in work and play:

Those whispering leaves behind the slit
On the cabin wall of childhood's dreaming
  **and becoming.**

[180]

His poetry can be tough and sad, wailing,

> Goatshit on gutted alley-ways
> and near-rooted huts of mud
> their peeling thatch a plaything
>     for the termites,

Though still young and active, he laments the approach of old-age, the lost opportunities and the shattered dreams for a new world.

> Now, we are old
> We too once climbed the rising slope
> With eager youthful feet.
> . . . . . . . . . . . . . . . . . . . . . . . . . . .
> Tell them, who climb the slopes
> We saw the first suns rise;
> The first suns set.

In spite of his strong attachment to the familiar sounds and places of his childhood, Adali-Mortty prays for a bond beyond him, of men, life, love, and the universe.

The strongest element in Adali-Mortty's poetry is his childhood which he evokes in almost every poem, with a remarkable nostalgia and pathos, creating within the vanished dream of the world of youth, the hopes and the desires of a tiring and turbulent world.

> In Mars and in the Moon, maybe
> Some day, the reach our grasp!

ALBERT KAYPER-MENSAH was born in Sekondi in 1923 and studied at Mfantsipim School, Wesley College and Achimota before taking a degree in Natural Science at Cambridge. After a Diploma Course in Education at London University he taught for a few years before joining the Ghana Foreign Service, holding posts in London and Bonn.

He started writing while at Cambridge "to keep and deepen my experiences from my Natural Science studies, of the oneness of life." He has had poems published in *Granta, Okyeame, Ghanaian Times, Neues Afrika* and *Afrika Heute,* as well as in *A Book of African Verse* (African Writers Series) and other anthologies. In 1957 he won the Margaret Wrong Literary Prize for a collection of poems. He has also won a British Council prize for one of his plays.

He writes of his poetry, "Personal friendship, open lectures, and the arts opened for me many doors of wider self-education in Cambridge. Proverb technique in Akan oral literature fascinated me and now, the more it inspires my writing, the more African I feel my writing is."

KOFI AWOONOR was born in Wheta in the Keta district of Ghana of a Ghanaian family whose ancestry stretches through Togo and Dahomey. He has published in 1964, *Rediscovery*, a volume of poetry, and another volume *Night of my Blood* is coming out soon. He has taught in College, researched in African Literature, acted on the stage, been Director of a film company, written for radio, and now lives in New York. He read at the Poetry Centre in New

York in June 1968 in the company of the Polish poet
Herbert and the French poet Guillevic. He is now visiting
professor in African literature, at State University of
New York, Stony Brook.

Kofi Awoonor's early poetry – published under the name
of George Awoonor-Williams – marks his apprenticeship
as a poet; this period saw him using and translating tradi-
tional poetry. The poems of this period – some of which are
included in Beier and Moore's *Modern Poetry from Africa* –
capture the songs and the funeral dirges of the Anlos.
What may be described as the second phase of his develop-
ment is marked by the poetry of *Night of my Blood*, and the
poems which are included in this volume. He says of this
phase: 'I have gone through the trauma of growth, anger,
love, and the innocence and nostalgia of my personal
dreams. These are beyond me now. Not anger, or love, but
the sensibility that shaped and saw them as communal acts
of which I am only the articulator. Now I write out my
renewed anguish about the crippling distresses of my
country and my people, of death by guns, of death by
disease and malnutrition, of the death of friends whose
lives held so much promise, of the chicanery of politics
and the men who indulge in them, of the misery of the
poor in the midst of plenty. What can you describe me? A
marxist? A communist, a dilettante? I am none of these.
I am a human being possessed of the normal sensibilities of
all human beings. Hence my songs. My self-recognition is
my personal redemption realized through so much that is
sad and destructive; I still cling on to hope for man,
African man, black, silent and vulnerable.'

AYI KWEI ARMAH, born in 1938, studied at Achimota,

Harvard and Legon, at present lives in Paris, and is on a Fellowship in the United States. Perhaps Ghana's most accomplished prose and fiction writer who has just published his first novel, *The Beautyful Ones Are Not Yet Born*. He is represented here by only one poem 'Aftermath'. This is a poem of a very personal nature, full of pleading and demands for understanding, a plea to be left alone.

Enjoy your freedom
Leave me,
Go.


KWESI BREW was born in 1928. Brew has had an exciting career as a Government Agent after Legon. In Ghana's diplomatic service he served in India and West Germany before becoming Ghana's first Ambassador to Mexico. He is at present accredited to Senegal. He has just published his first volume of poetry, *Shadows of Laughter* (Longmans, 1969.)

Brew's poetry is marked by his deep concern for the future of his country, a nostalgia for old traditional values. These are underlined by a deep love affair with a woman who is the symbol of all that he clings to and holds nearest his heart. His earlier poetry, some of which is included in this volume, is the poetry of maturity, search, anguish and restlessness.

Be gentle, be kind my beloved
for words become memories
and memories tools
in the hands of jesters.

Brew takes up the search for the past, for values that have vanished; he wondered whether to look:

In fear upon the past or to rejoice
But Brew's poetry is full of anguish
   The songs you asked me to sing
   I have sung them all
   On the desolate sands of my journey
   I have arrived O my Lord at your shrine
   But the peace you promised me stays
   In your heart beyond my reach.

In 'The Executioner's Dream', a grim apocalyptic vision of blood and torn membranes, the poet addresses a lover, a dispenser of wrath, a healer and a seer:–

   Horrors were your flowers then
   The bright red bouganvillea.
   They delighted you;
   Why do you weep
   And offer me this little gift
   Of a dull onyx set in a crown of thorns?

Brew's imagery is drawn from a large tableau of Christian and pagan concepts; his Christianity is the basis of his doubt; his belief in traditional ideals the anchor of his personal hopes. His poetry can be intensely personal; the intensity is marked by a certain hopelessness at man's destiny:

   But we have come in tattered penury
   Begging at the door of a master.

AMU DJOLETO was born in 1929. He has published a novel, *The Strange Man* (Heinemann 1967), and works as a Senior Official in the Ministry of Education in Accra. He describes himself as detribalized. He has been writing poetry for a long time. Apart from one poem 'The Lone Horse' which appeared in *Voices of Ghana*, this is his major appearance as a poet. His poetry is marked by a certain ambivalence, cynicism and a quiet acceptance, of arrogant outburst and gentle humility. Staid, level-headed and witty, he is at the same time restless:

I have taken the lead
And missed the sweet honey
A QUEST: I am not asking to be left on my own
It's a quest to be nearer a force my own

His is essentially the speaking voice, asking questions, demanding answers to unanswerable questions.

Should I blame myself or the Universe
Or is there nothing wrong but my verse
Why is it that it is even if I am a fool?

There is an earthiness about Djoleto's poetry that gives it a light-hearted conversational quality.

'And when everybody is naked, we shall all join in a global dance forgetting the old facile motto' is as far as he goes in wide eschatological gestures of global identity.

CAMERON DUODU was born in 1937 in Akyem Abuakwa, and is self-taught. He is one of Ghana's most talented journalists and author of the novel *The Gab Boys* (Deutsch). He is essentially a representative member of his generation of restless searching sensitive intellectual youth of Africa who are asking terrible questions and getting no intelligent answers from their elders who seem to be fouling up their dreams and hopes. In the few poems included in this anthology, Duodu's use of sarcasm is unsurpassed. In 'The Stranded Vulture' Duodu's use of sharp satire permeates every line:

And you natter and natter
Expecting the hungry bitch

[186]

To feed you rich
Oh vulture,
Silly creature,
I would laugh at you
Were it not so true
That – *I* made you.

'Echoes of Eden' is a nostalgic poem of childhood, the past of dreams and elemental nature in harmony with the technical bitchiness of the Ferrari, money, graphs and computers, and the external attributes of naïve humanity. In this poem, Duodu's feel for words, colours, and sounds supersedes his anger. Swift moves are made from love scenes to birds, to truancy, to cold technical imagination. The finale is gratitude

God, I am grateful to you
Oh God, I am so grateful.

ELLIS AYETEY KOMEY was born in 1927. His poetry first appeared in *Modern Poetry from Africa*, and he has edited with Ezekiel Mphahlele a collection of short stories from Africa.

Komey's verse runs the full course of personal poetry, and public verse. In his poem 'Oblivion', Komey's feel for things dying is part of his own death wish:

I want to remember them
Before they die and turn to mud
When I have gone

KOJO GYINAYE KYEI, was born in 1932. He was educated in America and is an architect by profession. He gave an exhibition of his painting in the summer of 1968 in London where he is doing further work on timber. His

[187]

first volume of poetry *The Lone Voice* (Ghana Universities Press, 1969) has recently been published. His is a variety of light-hearted poetry, humorous, and quaintly sniggering and the poetry of dead seriousness and doubt.

    Life the only
    Wayside inn
    On this
    Rough-and-tumble safari
    Every man jack
    Of our party
    Stops here overnight.
    After that,
    He is only
    A memory.

    KOFI SEY is a lecturer in English at the University of Ghana, Legon. This is his first appearance in anthology. He has published, with lyrics by his friend Ebenezer Laing, a libretto of verse and songs which was privately distributed among friends. Though his poetry is concerned with serious subjects, Sey has an infinite capacity for laughter; this is his forte as a writer:

    How dare you imply or say
    By those persistent questions
    That I lie in everything I say.

His laughter can be bitter:

    That's no matter – get up and
    Let's be going – all this is idle.

To say that Sey's verse is all laughter is to misjudge the basic tone of poetry that can cry, laugh, and weep tears

    With a single purpose
    To wait for the rain.

FRANK KOBINA PARKES is one of Ghana's major poets. He published a volume of poetry *Songs from the Wilderness* (1965). He has worked as a journalist all his life, and is now attached to the Ministry of Information in Accra. His imagery, like that of many of his contemporaries is drawn from Christianity and pagan rituals; the creates a world peopled by 'strange sights':

Stones shall be turned to men

. . . . . . . . . . . . . . . . . . . .

So children
If perchance you see a hare that roars
Or an ape perched in a palanquin
Look on in silence.

In a poem, 'Blind Steersmen', Parkes in a *cri de cœur* talks about self-defence, lost, as the world:

And I, blown by thick puffs of factory smoke
Mad neither for my sorrows nor the world's
Seek faith in the vision I know is false
In sanity I know is mere soul-effacement.

. . . . . . . . . . . . . . . . . . . .

The salvation of the world lies in a deserted Garden
In a blind worm's crawl.

Parkes has a tremendous feel for words and a control that is firm and meaningful.

Depths are frozen wombs
Barren skulls and cross bones picked
And earth belonged to other races – pressed in Steel.
To a land where, he cries,
The streams of life gush out in tuneful song
Dead bones in mansions moving
As the glory of God descends on earth
To be despoiled.

## BIOGRAPHICAL NOTES

EFUA THEODORA SUTHERLAND has very much been at the centre of Ghana's artistic life. She was the founder of the Ghana Drama Studio, and directed the first crop of traditional Ananse Plays. She has written a number of plays including *Edufa* (Longmans, 1968). Her concern with poetry and drama is to combine the genius of traditional forms with the techniques of the modern stage, and English language. She has written *The Roadmakers* and a number of children's books. Her greater concern at the moment is to provide reading for Ghanaian children, material to fill the void. She has started a village experimental theatre in the Central Region of Ghana.

E. A. WINFUL is a Principal Secretary in the Civil Service of Ghana. Educated in Ghana and in Britain, he is a quiet, cultured gentleman of few words and has the reputation of being a wit. This is reflected in his poetry, some of which appeared in *Okyeame*, the Ghanaian literary journal, in 1966.